LIFE OF A *Virtuous* WOMAN

WHEN GOD SPEAKS...

Pastor
GWENDOLYN
BOWEN, PhD.
&
OTHER WOMEN OF GOD

Elite
PUBLICATIONS

Living the Life of a Virtuous Woman: When God Speaks
by Pastor Gwendolyn Bowen, PhD.

Published by:
Elite Publications
2120 E Firetower Rd. # 107-58
Greenville, NC 27858
Tel: 919-618-8075
info@elitepublications.org
Visit us online at: www.elitepublications.org

LIBRARY OF CONGRESS CONTROL NO.: 2024920368

PAPERBACK ISBN-13: 978-1-958037-28-7

KINDLE & EBOOK ISBN: 978-1-958037-29-4

PRINTED IN THE UNITED STATES OF AMERICA

This book is dedicated to Mother Isabelle Knight Dickens, my mother, and the mother of my ten siblings. She was a living model of the Proverbs 31 woman. She was a wife, mother, daughter, sister, aunt, niece, and friend to many, but most importantly, she could be found to be a virtuous woman. Truly, having been blessed with seven daughters, they have all done virtuously, but she excelled them all.

ONTENTS

"Who can find a virtuous woman? For her price is far beyond rubies." -
Proverbs 31:10

ACKNOWLEDGEMENTS

To God be the Glory for entrusting such a task to me as women with purpose rose to the occasion and shared their most intimate and spiritual encounters in getting to know God.

To Jessie Bowen, my husband, thank you for always seeing the best in me. And to my darling daughter, Jessica Carollyn Phillips, for your hard work and patience, I say *I love you more!*

FOREWORD

BY REVEREND MARY E. HIGGS

This book, *Living the Life of a Virtuous Woman: When God Speaks*, showcases the journeys of women who have chosen to lead a virtuous life by sharing how their relationship with God has transformed their lives after hearing His voice is more straightforward than one might imagine, and it can happen without our awareness. God speaks to us in many ways, such as through an impression in our spirit, a passage of Scripture, or a prophetic dream. We were created to commune with God, and He wants us to draw near to Him to understand His will for our lives and know His heart. As explained by each writer, we must seek Jesus for salvation and strength in doing His will to be virtuous. We must also ask Him to guide us and display His will by spending time with Him in prayer and Bible reading each day. Virtue is not just about doing but also about being. It necessitates a change of heart and the desire to do what is right, which only God can give us. All we have to do is ask, and He is waiting for us!

Dr. Gwendolyn Bowen, founder of Women of Powerful Prayer (W.O.P.P.), shares instructions on enduring adversity by deepening our relationship with the Lord. Dr. Bowen is a role model for many believers, especially women facing insurmountable odds in their walk with the Lord.

Dr. Bowen has revealed through the writers in this book how one can become and remain confident in knowing that Jesus will never leave or forsake you. I, Reverend Mary E. Higgs, Dr. Bowen's friend, neither sugarcoat nor compromise the Word of God, nor do the writers in this book. I am confident that no one can ever read this book without becoming better equipped to handle the adversities that are sure to come in life. As you read this book and your Bible, I am sure you will find that you have encountered God. He will strengthen your testimony and give your journey in life an even greater meaning.

Rev. Mary E. Higgs

Rev. Mary E. Higgs, Certified Theologian (Cth)
5-Star Author of *From Challenges to Change*

NTRODUCTION

BY PASTOR GWENDOLYN BOWEN, PHD.

I know that my mother's smile from resurrection territory exudes her approval of this book, *Living the Life of a Virtuous Woman: When God Speaks*, knowing that her labor was not in vain. I'm sure she would have each of us to be mindful of the qualities of a virtuous woman. She is rare, valuable, trusted, reasonable, willing, motivated, diligent, resourceful, dedicated, and discerning. Wow, what stellates to fill! But in her soft and yet motherly voice, I can hear her saying, "Don't you all get discouraged, because I lived long enough to know that the Proverbs 31 woman is not a real woman, but she's a model of a woman being perfected into the image of God. And in all your goodness, know that you may not measure up to this woman; you can daily seek to be more like her."

Not only her teachings and modeling but those of other Christian women throughout my life as I've grown in grace and spiritual maturity with Christ, I've learned that a virtuous woman is strong and dignified. She is a woman of character and integrity. And yes, we draw our strength from the Lord so we might not be afraid. Afraid not of who we are nor whose we are. We have to be aware that eyes and ears are always upon us. Therefore, we must be clothed in beauty, both inner and outer. Because when we are beautiful at heart, we can be a blessing to those around us. I recall my mother instructing us to be mindful of how we treat others because we might just be entertaining an angel. Know that we can make a difference in the lives of others.

Living the life of a Virtuous Woman: When God Speaks brings about wisdom. You know right, and you know wrong. Therefore, the day and season of our lives necessitate us to be as Paul the Apostle when he said in Psalm 119:66-67:

"Teach me good judgment, wise and right discernment, and knowledge, for I have believed (trusted, relied on, and clung to) Your commandments."

A virtuous woman is a woman of discernment. We can make wise decisions in business and life when we are full of wisdom. Life for the virtuous woman, I believe, in this 21st century has not become more accessible with all of life's affordability. Still, it has become more challenging because of humanity's change regarding God's goodness. Remember, we strive to be daily, and life constantly brings distractions.

Let us take a self-examination.

1. *Are you trustworthy?* Can you be trusted with the big and little things? Are you dependable and have integrity? Do you follow through in what you say you will do, whether big or small? For those of you hoping for marriage in the future, think about it: how can you honor your husband before you even meet him? Relationally, mentally, spiritually?

2. *Are you one who sacrifices your time, energy, money, or other resources?* What are you working towards? As a mom, are you waking up with your kids? Are you getting up early and staying up late, working overtime, or giving up those things you desire to save money or put towards a necessity?

3. *Are you disciplined?* Are you diligent in taking care of your responsibilities and business? It is said she holds the distaff in her hands–the distaff keeps the fibers together. I believe that, in many ways, so does the virtuous woman, whether in her home or business.

4. *How often do you open your arms to those in need?* I love these words because they show that the virtuous woman is not just charitable. It shows that she welcomes, engages, shows concern, and feels empathy.

5. *Are you tidy/neat?* Now, you may not necessarily be trendy or wear Lui Vuitton, but you can surely maintain your appearance, clothes, and home appearance. I've learned that being approachable in appearance tends to affect other areas of your life and your relationships. There's an old saying: a tidy house makes for a clear mind. And I'm sure that just this little tidbit, if received wisely, you'll find there's space to get your work done, you're able to run your household more efficiently, you'll have a desire to entertain, and yes, you'll welcome the time to meditate, more time spent with God.

6. *How do you make your husband feel?* I can attest that a husband who does well in life usually has a supportive wife. True Christianity means that we consider the other's interests above our own. And yet, husbands, you must also love, sacrifice for, and walk as Jesus does. And I hear both the husband and wife asking, why? Truthfully, I don't know the answer to your whys, but I do know that God designs relationships in an orderly way. Jesus is described as submissive in the Bible, and we would never consider Him to be a doormat, a sidekick, or less powerful.

7. *Are you watchful of your words?* The virtuous woman is kind and wise in her speech, not a gossiper on the cellphone or texting half the day, for he says of her, "She openeth her mouth with wisdom, and in her tongue is the law of kindness." The law of kindness

does not rule gossip but a speech we would not use against ourselves.

8. *Just how blessed are you?* The virtuous woman is blessed, and her children shall rise and call her blessed; her husband also praises her. Many a great man has turned to bless his mother and speak her praises, as did Abraham Lincoln when he said, "All that I am and hope to be, I owe to my angel mother."

Ladies, we are purposed with a great assignment. As you can see, this woman is strong, dignified, unhurried, and unworried. She is wise and faithful.

As we press forward, let us join hand in hand, for we are onward Christian soldiers marching as to war, with the cross of Jesus going on before. Christ the royal Master leads against the foe, forward into battle see His banner go – for we wrestle not against flesh and blood, but against principalities, against powers, against the rulers of the darkness of this world, against spiritual wickedness in high places (Ephesians 6:12).

I pray that you and I will seek to impress upon ourselves more of the characteristics of the Proverbs 31 woman. We will become more focused and empowered to leave our virtuous imprints in the lives of others as we sojourn, leaving our imprints in the sands of time. May we purpose to be better for our family, husband, children, and friends.

Who can find a Virtuous Woman? *Is it I? Is it I? Is it I?*

"Being confident of this very thing, that he which hath begun a good work in you will perform it until the day of Jesus Christ:"
Philippians 1:6

Pastor Gwendolyn Bowen

Pastor Gwendolyn Bowen, PhD.
International Best-Selling Author
Operations Editor at Elite Publications
www.MinisterGwenBowen.com

WHEN ALL ELSE
FAILS

CHAPTER 1

KEPT ON PURPOSE FOR A PURPOSE

BY REVEREND GLADYS SMITH

It all began in August 1997 when I was about to cross an item off my bucket list. I flew nine hours to Honolulu, Hawaii. The first two days were amazing, but the morning of the third day was a nightmare. I woke from my sleep with excruciating pain, and as I tried to stand, the pain worsened. I could not walk down the steps without tears rolling down my cheeks due to the pain.

My son, who was stationed in Hawaii with the military, bought me over-the-counter meds, and by evening, I began to feel better. The next day, I was able to walk with only slight pain. I was thankful that the pain was subsiding, but where did it come from? I finished my two-week stay in Hawaii and was able to enjoy it as long as I took the pain medications. Upon my return home on Thursday morning, I was not pain-free, but it was much better.

I proceeded to get back into my routine, and I felt good. My family and I went to church Sunday morning, and it seemed all was well. After being gone for two weeks, I got out of the daily cooking routine, so I got in my car to grab food for dinner. I never made it out of the driveway. As I tried to turn the key in my car ignition, I felt like every bone in my wrist was to the point of breaking. I thought to myself, what in the world is going on with me? I made it through the rest of Sunday.

Monday morning, I called my doctor to see if I could get an appointment to find the source of my pain. The doctor's visit didn't go very well. They suggested it was all in my head as my lab results were within normal limits. My SED rate was average, meaning I did not have arthritis. My doctor prescribed me pain meds and sent me on my way.

Well, several weeks went by, and the pain persisted. One day at work, I felt like the bones in my knees were going to break, so I went back to my doctor. At this point, my doctor made a referral to a rheumatologist. I went to the rheumatologist, who looked at my face and said I had a butterfly rash. I thought, what is that? It is a rash that patients who are diagnosed with Lupus often get. The rheumatologist looked at me and said I'm 99% sure that you have Systemic Lupus Erythematosus. I learned that there are four major types of Lupus, but this one is known to affect the joints.

I didn't know that much about the disease even though I had been working in healthcare for years. The rheumatologist explained that the disease was an autoimmune disease that could affect any major body organ. It all sounded like a death sentence. I listened attentively, and at the end of the conversation, I heard, "There is no cure for the disease."

Panic gripped my very core. Are you telling me I'm not going to be here to see my youngest son graduate from high school? To see my grandkids grow up and graduate from high school? I just cannot accept that.

On a Monday morning, I received a call from the rheumatologist requesting that I come into the office to discuss the results of my latest tests. It was confirmed. I did have Systemic Erythematous Lupus, which is an autoimmune disease that affects the joints in the body. With this diagnosis, one can have what has been determined as flare-ups. From my experience, when a flare-up occurs, it is almost as if your life has to be put on hold. The everyday tasks cannot be completed, and you cannot be of help to yourself, much less anyone else.

I went through some dark days of taking much pain medication to get me through the day. At my lowest point, I was taking 27 pills a day to keep me functioning. I was on massive doses of steroids, and my face looked like a Pillsbury dough lady. At my lowest point, I considered going to the lake in my neighborhood and jumping in. I just could not take the pain!

I questioned God about why this was happening to me. Since Lupus can be hereditary, I searched my family history only to discover that no one in my family has ever been diagnosed with Lupus. I had a pity party with myself, but then I cried out to the Lord, and he heard my cry.

As I cried out to the Lord, He led me to a scripture in the Bible that I still quote today. It was Isaiah 53:5, which says, "But he was wounded for our transgressions, he was bruised for our iniquities: the chastisement of our peace was upon him, and with his stripes, we are healed."

I began to have a serious conversation with the Lord. I asked him, "God, how do I handle this diagnosis?" He said to have faith and believe in Him. So, I prayed, I fasted, and I trusted God. I had to lean on him because there was really nothing else that I could do.

In the midst of my trials, I had been trying to discover my true purpose in life. I had a good job, a wonderful family, and a circle of good friends, but deep inside, I knew God's plan included more for me.

I had many dark days, many absences from work, many visits to the emergency department, several inpatient hospital visits, and test after test after test. Somewhere along the path, God's Word took on life for me. I also began to quote the scripture, Psalm 118:17, *I shall not die, but live, and declare the works of the Lord.*

During my trials with Lupus, I began to cry out to the Lord like never before. I had been going to church and believing in God for many years, but I realized I didn't have a personal one-on-one relationship with him. I realized that going to church did not make me immune to trials. As I moved forward, I began to study the Word more to see what God wanted for me.

I prayed earnestly that God would show me my true purpose through my sufferings. As I studied the Word daily, I felt peace within myself. I learned how to control the pain from the Lupus and not let it control me. I knew that God would never put more on me than I could bear!

As I studied God's Word and openly confessed my faith in Him, I began telling others what I knew He could do for them. I told them to trust and believe in God no matter how dark things seem. I began to tell them that God shows no favoritism, so they needed to start speaking those things as though they already manifested.

I joined the local North Carolina Lupus Association and was an active participant as I shared my story. I participated in several of the annual Lupus walks. I spoke at our local college, providing information and hope to those who were going through challenging situations in their lives. It may not have been Lupus, but it was something that they could not fix by themselves. I began to share that no matter how difficult the situation, things could turn around, and the sun would shine again.

One day, as I was speaking to my friend's cousin, who had recently been diagnosed with a horrible disease, God showed me what my true purpose in life was. I was so excited because I now knew that God wanted me to use my story as a testimony to help others. I felt good inside but also a little overwhelmed that He had chosen me to be a mouthpiece for Him. He had chosen me to go through suffering and pain because he knew that I could handle it and would not give up.

Usually, I am very shy, but as I began to speak to different people and tell of the goodness of God, a boldness started to rise in me. I was not timid in sharing that not only is God a healer, but He is a keeper. I was excited and overcame my shyness as I proclaimed that faith in God can move any mountain. You see, I knew that as my faith in God grew, the Lupus trials had decreased. The flare-ups decreased, and the pain meds and doctor visits decreased.

So here I am, almost 28 years later, still surviving the diagnosis of Systemic Lupus Erythematosus. I am a living witness that everything will turn out for your good if you trust God. His Word says that He will never leave nor forsake us (Deuteronomy 31:6). He also said that we could cast all of our cares on Him, for He cares for us (1 Peter 5:7).

So, I continue to fight this horrible disease. I continue to lean on Jesus as He is my source. He is my everything. My personal time with Jesus Christ grew through this terrible ordeal. I developed a very personal relationship with God, and in April 2018, God saw fit to call me into the ministry. He wanted me to be a mouthpiece for him.

I was not sure that I could handle this huge responsibility. There are so many negative comments about women preachers and them being unqualified. I cried out to the Lord and said, "Lord, if this is what you want me to do, show me a sign, and I will do it." We all know that God doesn't need to prove himself to anybody, but He did show me that I had been called. Through a dream, He showed me at the altar in an all-white attire, speaking in another language, praying for the saints, and laying my hands on them to be healed. The dream was so real that I woke wet with sweat and cried out to the Lord. At that very moment, I began to cry out, saying, "Yes, Lord. I will go where you tell me to go and say what you want me to say."

As I said yes to God, He let me know that everyone I thought loved me would not be happy for me, nor would they support me. He admonished me not to let this hinder my journey because more would come to replace those who left. As I embarked on this new journey, the light bulb came on, and I knew that I didn't need a big entourage as long as I had Jesus.

Soon after I accepted the call and began to boldly stand and declare His Word, I realized that God had kept me on purpose for a purpose. That purpose was to be his servant. Wherever I go today, I must boldly declare the wages of sin is still death, but the gift of God is still eternal life. I must tell everyone that I meet that Heaven and Hell are real, and when they die, they will go to one or the other.

I must encourage those who have made mistakes and let them know that no one is perfect.

As I continue to be a mouthpiece for Him, I must spend some time with the youth and let them know that it's okay not to fit in with the crowd, it's okay to go to church and participate in the worship experience, and it's always okay to stand up for doing right.

As I prepare to lay my pen aside, I am forever grateful to God for keeping me for my purpose. Am I perfect? No. Do I make mistakes? Yes. Are some days still a struggle? Yes, but I will continue to praise God.

Lastly, as I encourage you, I encourage myself: Let's continue to walk by faith. Tell the story that faith is the key to unlocking many doors.

Because I am healed and I now know that I can do all things through Christ, I must cry loud and tell the story of how Jesus saves, heals, and sets the captives free. You can do all things through him, too.

Until the Lord leads me to pick up my pen, I will pray that you continue to stand on God's Word and be led by him.

You, my friends, are overcomers. BE HAPPY!

REVEREND GLADYS SMITH
DEVOTIONAL

EXPECTATIONS

"In the morning, O Lord, You hear my voice: in the morning, I lay my requests before You and wait in expectation." (Psalm 5: 3)

It takes a lot of faith to hope and even more to expect. But you can do both when it comes to faith and your prayers. It's not that you will always pray for a specific thing and get it, like placing a catalog order online. But what you can expect when you lay your concerns before God is that He will answer. Your prayers do not have to fall on disregarding ears. You can count on that. Jesus promised His return. He expects you to live with the certainty that He will return soon and to live your life accordingly.

Prayer:

My hope, Lord, is built on nothing less than Your word and Your righteousness. I live in each day knowing that You will return for me one day. Grant unto me your Holy Spirit that I might be able to recognize the times and the seasons. I might be able to live with the certainty that You will return soon, and I might have accomplished my purpose. *Amen*

ABOUT
*G*LADYS SMITH

Gladys Smith is a retired HIMS (Health Information Management Services) professional. She worked at a major hospital in Eastern North Carolina for over thirty years.

Gladys has a heart for helping others, especially older people and children.

Gladys is one of her church's associate ministers and is involved in various church functions. She serves as the Superintendent of Sunday School, assists with monthly food bank distributions, sings in the choir, is a board member and secretary of the church foundation, and readily assists with other duties the pastor may assign.

Gladys loves to write, read, exercise, and cook. She recently started a small baking and soul food cooking business and enjoys serving and feeding others in her free time.

$\mathcal{J}$UMP SHIP & TRUST GOD

BY DR. MARSHA D. WILLIAMS

The melodic version of this story is fiddling around pain. An obliterating pain not even pride could ignore. This is the kind of pain that prohibits anything else except being in pain (and doing anything to alleviate it). When all else fails, I have to let go. In letting go, I fearfully learned my pain had been created for a purpose.

I grew up in an environment where seeds were planted in a field of dreams. This cultivation allowed me to grow in a garden created for a purpose. What could be my purpose? Why was I created? As an only child, I was born six years after my parents were married. The birth of a baby girl to two gainfully employed professionals would seem like a perfectly illustrated family: a two-parent family home. My father was an amazingly humble, honorable military man and one of Chicago's finest officers. Isadore Jr., also known as Sonny, was the most patient man I knew. My mother, an astounding woman with a heart of giving, Margaret, also known as Peggy, worked as a compassionate nursing administrator in healthcare and education.

I am a "Daddy's Girl." Sonny was a man of great wisdom, integrity, and courage. When it comes to my father, I know I inherited his positive traits, and I would like to think that when all else fails, my father will lead with love. Out of love, I watched my father endure great pain. I watched my father be a husband, a son, and a functional alcoholic. He was my first hero. I formed relationship goals by watching my father. The first human relationship God created was Adam and Eve. Adam was not meant to be alone. "It is not good for the man to be alone. I will make a helper suitable for him." Genesis 2:18(NIV) My parents were amazing; they modeled my firsthand love story.

As I grew older, I learned more about our first love story in the Bible. I'm unsure how long it was from the time that God created Adam until He purposely created Eve. There are a few verses between the time Adam was made and when God pulled a rib from Adam and created Eve. As an adult Christian, I wonder how long God allowed Adam to be alone. There is no failure in God. With that in mind, my parents were married for thirty-seven years when my father died in 2001. I recall my father spending a lot of his time in reflection. Taking his life back from abusing alcohol and seventeen years of sobriety, Sonny needed someone to talk to, just like Adam.

My mother plowed the flowers of my heart with sacrifice and protection. In 1980, I was informed that luck was why I was created. My mother told me, "You're lucky you got here; your daddy wanted kids, I didn't." Not only was I informed that my mother didn't want kids, but my father wanted a boy. When someone makes sacrifices for something, this could reward them in the future. This reward is God's favor. Often, the great thing about sacrifice is that it is temporary. Whatever my mother may have sacrificed in giving birth to me in 1970, it was temporarily preparing for my purpose and filling my heart with the spirits of release and forgiveness.

There are people in your life who will lift you up and support you whenever you need it. And there may be others who delight in tearing you down or causing you pain.

I learned this well from my maternal family. Their actions aren't isolated events but behavior patterns that negatively shaped my life.

I asked myself, "Why do you hold on to this negativity?" For whatever reasons, I'm inclined to believe that my thought process back then was somehow, my transgressors would suffer as well. We grow up thinking, "We're only human," which means we make mistakes. We may also do potentially damaging things for others or even ourselves (maybe even unintentionally). Our impulse should be to do better and make things right. Instead, holding on to negativity, guilt, anger, or shame is like Gorilla Glue®, binding us to those circumstances that wrong us and prolonging our escape. Holding on to those negative memories only allowed me to create more of the same. I became a victim of my memories, not the people who betrayed me.

Nevertheless, the way God created us, we can't pick and choose who we will or will not forgive. Forgiveness is a significant movement towards spiritual healing, and it requires me to think from the heart and not from my head. In my head, I was angry, hurt, and unconsciously out of harmony with my mission in life. When all else fails, respond with God-like forgiveness.

Your feelings may go beyond displeasure if you've experienced a toxic family dynamic. Instead of interacting with or even thinking about my family, I chose to ignore any painful experiences. I had always taken those painful experiences and made them intentionally personal. Even though it caused significant emotional distress, I know now it was intended to stretch my faith and my patience. Growing up, I wondered if God loved me, and sometimes, my pain had me wondering if God was out there somewhere. This world consumes us by trying to meet the expectations set by unrealistic standards. My maternal family's expectations were painful. As a child, I spent my summers in the suburbs of Chicago. I'm so glad trouble doesn't always last. Coming from a two-parent home provided me with two different outlets; the difference was as the light is to darkness.

I was around eight or nine when I had to figure out a way to remove myself from a toxic environment. Any environment of sexual abuse perpetrated against anyone is the deplorable reality we often face today, living in a sin-stricken world. Unfortunately, that was my reality, and I wouldn't say I liked it. Remember, I'm a "Daddy's Girl." He taught me that communication is important. Discussing with him my moments of toxicity, what he shared with me would allow me to give up anger or fear so that I was able to give in to change.

It would seem that those who molest/fondle children may have been hurt in some way as well; perhaps they choose to victimize other children in an attempt to regain their sense of power or worthiness. The Holy Spirit revealed their misguided attempt to find themselves was not my place to figure out why this was happening to me. Nevertheless, sexual abuse is evil, and I quickly felt I was safer at home with Mom and Dad or at my grandmother's house. At my grandmother's house, a spiritual connection was attempting to teach me how to live as a virtuous woman. Strong, beautifully spirited, and proud entrepreneurial women lived in my grandmother's home. A home that tried its best to usher me into becoming a virtuous woman. Imagine a house with ample space to create: nine bedrooms, three bathrooms, and a finished basement. They taught me that the Holy

Spirit is indifferent to good or bad. I was placed in a safe environment where accountability was universal. I experienced a fantastic childhood every season that followed. Attending a Catholic elementary school and a Catholic all-girls high school, I was looking forward to leaving my parents' home and attending a university. Completely away from my family, I began to learn about spirituality.

Fast forwarding through my college years, 1988 to 1990 were fun and full of sin. I was free as a bird. Thank God He keeps His eye on the sparrow; He indeed kept His eyes on me. This world was consuming me solely because of the poor choices I made. I lived according to my will and unconsciously experienced spiritual and emotional welfare. Not knowing my fate, I invited the spoils of this world into my life and forgot the source of my joy. I physically walked away from that place where God lived within me, and I lived through Him, knowing my value and my worth.

Nevertheless, anything and everything I have experienced was purposeful. In 1990, I left Alabama State University to chase after a man. The next seven years of my life will soon reveal the purpose of my pain. There were several moments when I was more scared than I've ever been in my life. Alcoholism, to me, was like drinking water. I witnessed my dad live as a functional alcoholic; therefore, my pride led me to believe I was a functional drug addict. I took on spirits that tried to kill me daily. I know I have not lost anything or anyone within the divine orders of my life. I was being molded into the Creator's perfect expression of now Dr. Marsha D. Williams.

Because of my struggle with intimacy and secrecy, isolation came easy. When all else fails, tell the truth and shame the devil. During my drug addiction, I became the very reality I've judged or ridiculed. I was searching for that first high, a feeling of pleasure, and I wanted to numb my pain. My soul was not connected to the Holy Spirit's presence and purpose until God called me. God is omniscient (all-knowing), omnipresent (everywhere present), omnipotent (all-powerful), and His love never fails or dies! He saved me one lonely night in Chicago.

It was a Friday night, I just got paid, and I'm sure I was thinking or humming Johnny Kemp's song. I cashed my check at the currency exchange and ran off to find one of the corner boys. I searched everywhere. That night, I couldn't find a corner boy in sight until I ran into another dope fiend. This was perfect (or so I thought); he knew other spots and instructed me to follow him—one of the scariest moments in my life. I wasn't thinking about that. We walked to an apartment building where the guy I was excited to see gave another guy I didn't know my money. Then, the three of us walked to an abandoned lot where an abandoned car was sitting. I wasn't at all scared then- I just wanted to get high. Even my pride would not allow me to be scared. I was tough, so I thought, but I now know the omnipresent Spirit covered me.

The guy we met up with opened the door to the abandoned car, and he got in; the other guy told me to get in, and I sat in the middle of two strangers in an abandoned lot inside of an abandoned car, and all I wanted to do was get high; I wasn't thinking about anything else. One of the guys started to get high; the other guy started getting high. All I could do was sit there thinking my money was going up in smoke. I'm sitting in the middle of two strangers, thinking to myself, *"Hey, y'all smoking my dope! That's not how I do it; man, y'all wasting it!"* Before I could think twice, I said out loud, "I just want what I paid for." The one guy who we went and got from the apartment was sitting to the left, and the other guy to the right. The guy sitting on my left pulled out a gun.

As I looked at him, holding a gun, he had it pointed at me. Fear then consumed me! I sat there in the heart of the South Side of Chicago; no one in my family knew where I was, and no one in that car knew me personally. But I was on the verge. I was at a low point where I was hungry for that next high, on the verge of losing my dignity and self-respect. I was at that point where I had lost all sense of my reality, and I knew I was about to die. I heard the guy on my left say, "I feel like killing somebody tonight." I consciously remember deep breathing, breathing in and out, and through my peripheral vision, I saw a light to the right of me exiting the car. Both those guys were strangers to me. I didn't know either one of their names, and they didn't know who I was. It was at this moment I realized who I was! I realized at that moment when I took my deep breath, it became my beacon of life that allowed the Holy Spirit to move through that obstacle and regain my power in Christ Jesus! That breath was my source and my strength. The Great I Am was there; with that in mind, I understand that nothing happens in life without breath. And, when all else fails, breathe, and remember that God is in total control.

I couldn't tell you what those men looked like, but as the man on my right opened his door and got out, I slid out of the car after him. I walked away from that abandoned lot without my money or my drugs. The keywords are I walked away, The very essence of God's plan lives inside each of us. However, the enemy thought he had me in a chokehold. Thank God I had a praying father; you see, my father picked me up and took me to the currency exchange. Plus, God watches over fools. (Psalms 116:6) I have always kept a job. I was making good money, but I stayed broke. I was spending my money on dope. Friends were digressing, I wasn't using my own talents, and I was tired of struggling, so I stopped. Just that quickly, things changed.

The same night I evaded those evil spirits, God was sending me a ram in the bush. As I was walking away from the danger, I prayed: "*Lord, if you get me back home to my mother and father, I'll tell them I have a drug problem and I need help.*" Immediately after, a lady walked up to me, asking me if I needed a bus transfer. Back then, the Chicago Transit Authority (CTA) utilized transfers, and I needed two rides to get home to my parents. Two rides are what was left on this lady's transfer. As I looked down at the transfer and noticed the two rides, I instantaneously looked back up to thank her, but she was nowhere to be found. I looked East and West, but there was no one. North of me was a wall, and South of me was an empty street. Where did she go? I suppose she used her wings on her next assignment from Heaven.

Despite the pain and suffering I may have experienced during those seasons, I've learned to experience it all through hope and encouragement. My refusal to succumb to despair embodies my resilience and fierce spirit. I recognize now that I have an anointing power, and my ministry to serve began earlier than I had anticipated for my purpose in Christ Jesus. My spirit was building its resilience and inner strength. Although I often proclaim radical change, possibly even portrayed in a defiant spirit, I know now it was by faith that I was refusing to be defeated by life's challenges. We all know instinctively that there is virtue in courageous resolve. Undoubtedly, however, it must be the right kind. My courage-building confidence led me to a conviction of a sacrifice more significant than myself. As an only child, I grew up learning how to stand up to evil for the sake of righteousness. My kind of courage became intuitively evident that in me lived true greatness: dying to self for the sake of others.

Living life as a virtuous woman comes at a cost; I've learned that my every breath, thought, or word uttered is a prayer. Pride, selfishness, anger, jealousy, resentment, hatred, fear, and other toxic spirits stand in the way of prayer. God is the only entity we don't have to beg or bargain with; He always answers our prayers. Don't pray in doubt, for this cancels out the request. When all else fails, thank the Lord in ALL things, rebuke anything contrary to your faith, and stand firm. Pray with faith, knowing and believing what you ask for, which you already have. Breathe!

Take this time to make God the object of your affection, your path's destination, and your heart's goal. The goal is to have a heart of Jesus. Realize that God is the answer to whatever you are craving in your heart for life, for success, contentment, and truth. Seek the truth at all costs. Nothing you can do apart from God will mean anything; the time is now.

When all else fails, jump ship and trust God; swim to shore because you will find God there.

DR. MARSHA D. WILLIAMS
DEVOTIONAL

*L*OVE

"A new commandment I give you, love ye one another as I have loved you, so you must love one another. By this all men will know that you are my disciples, if you love one another." (John 13:34-35)

God loves you! Our human understanding can't comprehend the reason why, but only that it's true. God loves you relentlessly, completely, and in spite of your flaws and shortcomings. And yes, His greatest desire is for you to love in the same way. He asks us to love Him first in return and then to love others. Know that when you love, you show that you are His child; you demonstrate who you are and Whom you belong to. That pleases Him. Always live to please Him by loving others.

Prayer:

Jesus, teach me to love unconditionally, just as You love me. For You gave me the greatest gift, Your life! Thanks for loving me! *Amen.*

ABOUT
*M*ARSHA D. WILLIAMS

I am saved by Grace and living for the glory of Christ Jesus!

I accepted my calling to minister in 2022; I now oversee a "Traveling Ministry" as a Christian counselor, travel agent, life coach, motivational speaker, and indie film producer.

As a published author, I'm a faithful follower of Christ, spreading love and light!

TO KNOW

HIM

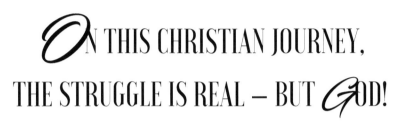ON THIS CHRISTIAN JOURNEY, THE STRUGGLE IS REAL – BUT GOD!

BY PASTOR GWENDOLYN BOWEN, PHD.

God is good! On this Christian journey, life does not always present itself positively.

If I could summarize my life in just five words and what the pursuit of what I want it to be about, there's a struggle because I still live in a sinful world. Still, if I could summarize my life into just five words about what I want my life to be about, those five words would be love, faith, trust, forgiveness, and hope.

The beauty of understanding a healthy Christian isn't that your life is absent from sin. We will always struggle with that. It's what you do with that sin once you recognize it in your life. See, some people will be content just living in it repeatedly, and they'll justify it by saying, "Well, everyone else sins." A true believer whose pursuit in life is to know God. I want to know Him. I've seen the magnitude of God's love displayed for me to the point He gave His life for my sin. It's a challenge, but I strive daily to choose not to grab ahold of those things that will separate me from Him. God, I want to know You.

Because of life's challenges and our being influenced by others, we somehow find ourselves trying to live the Christian life by a set of rules: "Do this, don't do that." "Do this, this, and this, but don't do that, that, or that." Many people view the Christian life as just a list of do's and don'ts. God has given us something better than rules, better than a formula, better than experience. God has given us the Holy Spirit. The Holy Spirit is the secret of living the Christian life. If you want to know where the Christian life is found and how to live in victory, then you must learn how to live by and through the Holy Spirit of God. That is the secret.

So, how is the Holy Spirit working in your life? Somebody said it's the difference between being in a car or on an elevated train. A car runs on the principle of storage. You put gas in the tank, and you drive it. You burn the gas, and when you're out of gas, you stop, get more gas, burn it, get more gas, and keep driving until you run out. You're constantly running and stopping and filling and refilling. On the other hand, an elevated train runs on the contact principle. You have the two rails on the outside and the electrified third rail in the middle. What is it that keeps the elevated train going? If the train stays in contact with that third rail in the middle, it will go and never stop.

Which are you? Too many people think that walking with the Holy Spirit is like riding in a car. You get filled with the Holy Spirit, and you get run down, then you get filled up again, to get run down again. So, they're constantly up and down, up and down, being filled and emptied, being filled and emptied. I'm learning that that's not the Christian life of the New Testament.

The New Testament tells us that the Holy Spirit is always present. Our job is to stay in contact with Him. When we do, He continuously provides the power we need for practical Christian living. There are two ways and only two ways of living in this world. You can live according to the flesh, which leads to death, or according to the Spirit, which leads to life. There is no third alternative; it's one or the other.

My parents instilled in me and my siblings at an early age that there was only one way, the right way, which was living for Jesus Christ. So, as a believer in Christ, I want you to know Him for yourself. I understand that life can bring some trying times, but I don't want you to quit. I want us to realistically look at the fact that we're in a sinful world, and at some point, in some way, someone you know will disappoint you. I don't walk with the expectation of perfection, but I want to encourage us to recognize the battles against sin and the pursuit that will stray us from knowing Him. The point isn't to stop doing wrong and start doing good. The fact is to turn from that and pursue His heart. Pursue God's heart.

And yes, if you know Jesus Christ, it ought to make a difference in every area of life. The way you speak, the way you talk, the way you write, the way you relate, and yes, the way you make decisions in the public arena. If you know Jesus Christ, that will radically affect the way you approach the great moral decisions of life. For too long, we who have been given new minds have been too willing to check them at the door as we leave church on Sunday morning. We think like pagans during the week but like Christians on Sunday morning. No wonder the world is a little impressed with our Christianity. They've never seen the real thing in action. What a difference it would make if we began to "think Christianly" and "act Christianly" in the workplace this week.

Job 14:1 says, "Man that is born of woman is of few days, and full of trouble." This life, as we know it, will one day no longer be. You're going to die someday, and your family and loved ones will attend your funeral. They'll go out to the grave, have a nice service, and lower your casket into the ground. They'll say some words, maybe sing a song, level off the dirt, and later put up the headstone. Then they'll go back to the church and have dinner. But (and this is a huge but) when they put you in the ground, that's not the end. If you know Jesus Christ, that's only the beginning.

Sometimes, we think that salvation means nothing more than going to heaven. But it's not as if you are some spiritual ghost. No. By virtue of God's promises, the work of Jesus Christ, and the indwelling Holy Spirit, when you die, you will not stay dead forever. You will one day experience a glorious resurrection. We have the promise that if God raised his Son Jesus from the dead, He will, by that same Spirit, raise you from the dead.

You and I were given a new mind to make a difference for God. God gave us a new mind so we could be a difference-maker for the kingdom of God.

As you walk with Him, He grows your heart and your love for people. In living out this will, you might consider the Apostle Paul and how God used him to transform the known world. And yes, God will meet you where you are.

Jesus spoke to Paul in the middle of his prosecution journey. He didn't wait for him to have a change of heart first. God called out to him while Paul traveled the dusty dirt roads with filth covering his feet and heart. God meets us where we are, too. We don't have to get cleaned up before we can meet our Savior. While we're lying in filth, we can call out to our sweet Jesus.

After Paul's conversion, the people were amazed. The same man who had hunted down Christians now called people to follow Jesus.

One of the greatest obstacles in ministry is also one of the greatest joys in ministry. While the greatest joy in ministry is people, sometimes the greatest obstacle is people because we all wrestle with sin. There's a challenge there for us. We are all imperfect. We are sinners saved by grace; therefore, we are at war with ourselves. Just like Paul, we also have a story to share. Others can benefit from hearing our tales of conversions and how God has worked out painful situations in our lives for God. God wants us to share these stories, teaching others about Christ and his salvation. We have the same Holy Spirit Paul had. We can use this power to bring others to Christ.

When I think about Paul's suffering, I think of Paul's saying in 2 Corinthians 12:7, "To keep me from exalting myself, there was given me a thorn in the flesh, a messenger of Satan to torment me, to keep me from exalting myself. Concerning this, I implored the Lord three times that it might leave me, and he said to me my grace is sufficient for you, for power is perfected in weakness. Most gladly, therefore, I would rather boast about my weakness that the power of Christ may dwell in me. Therefore, I am content with weakness, insults, distress, persecutions, and difficulties for the sake of Christ. For when I am weak, then I am strong."

Yes, your physical flesh is slowly wasting away. Yet God has placed life—eternal life, resurrection life—on the inside through the Holy Spirit. Dying on the outside, yet new life on the inside. We die, yet we live. We waste away, yet we live forever—seeds of life spring up where death once reigned. Though our bodies perish, our Spirit lives on with God. That's the wonder of the gospel. Where death once reigned, life now reigns within.

Are you keeping in contact with the Holy Spirit? Your job—your only real job as a Christian—is to stay in contact with the Spirit.

Day by day

Hour by hour

Moment by moment.

Let's talk about you and the Holy Spirit for a moment. How well have you been staying in contact?

Remember, there are only two ways to live—in the flesh or in the Spirit. There is no third option. Either you follow the dictates of your flesh—and the sinful pull it exerts, or you follow the Holy Spirit of God—which leads you in paths of righteousness. Who have you been following? What power have you been living by?

As we continue to enjoy this GREAT life God has given us, let us be mindful **that God wants us to know Him**.

Christianity is not just about knowing about God, knowing certain doctrines, or following certain moral precepts. It is essentially to know God. Jesus said (John 17:3), "This is eternal life, that they may know You, the only true God, and Jesus Christ whom You have sent." Christianity at its heart is, knowing God personally through Jesus Christ, who revealed God to us. If you do not know Him, you are not a Christian, no matter how correct your doctrine or how faithful your church attendance is. You may have been raised in the church, and you may have always adhered to Christian morality. But if you do not know God personally, you are not saved.

How well do you know Him?

Can you bear witness as the hymn writer Alan Jackson and say,

> *I serve a risen Savior; He's in the world today*
>
> *I know that He is living; whatever men may say*
>
> *I see His hand of mercy; I hear His voice of cheer*
>
> *And just the time I need Him, He's always near*
>
>
> *He lives! He lives! Christ Jesus lives today!*
>
> *He walks with me and talks with me*
>
> *Along life's narrow way*
>
> *He lives! He lives! Salvation to impart!*
>
> *You ask me how I know He lives.*

He lives within my heart.

In all the world around me, I see His loving care

And though my heart grows weary, I never will despair

I know that He is leading thro' all the stormy blast

The day of His appearing will come at last

He lives! He lives! Christ Jesus lives today!

He walks with me and talks with me

Along life's narrow way

He lives! He lives! Salvation to impart!

You ask me how I know He lives.

He lives within my heart.

Rejoice, rejoice, O Christian! Lift up your voice and sing

Eternal hallelujahs to Jesus Christ, the King!

The Hope of all who seek Him, the Help of all who find

None other is so loving, so good and kind

He lives! He lives! Christ Jesus lives today!

He walks with me and talks with me

Along life's narrow way

He lives! He lives! Salvation to impart!

You ask me how I know He lives?

He lives within my heart.

Oh, to know Him!

PASTOR GWENDOLYN BOWEN
DEVOTIONAL

DECISIONS

"The human mind plans the way, but the Lord directs the steps." (Proverbs 16:9)

It's always good to have a plan. And yet, it's also good to acknowledge that plans change. Make your list, set your priorities, and work them well. But do not forget to take the time to remember to surrender them to God. When you receive Christ, you are regenerated spiritually. The Spirit of God makes His home in you. You have the mind of Christ. As you quiet yourself and learn to hear the mind of Christ within you, you will find that your way becomes clearer.

Prayer:

Lord, create in me a clean heart. Renew my mind that I might be knowledgeable of your Spirit that dwells within me. *Amen.*

ABOUT
*G*WENDOLYN BOWEN

Pastor Dr. Gwendolyn Bowen is the Operations Editor for Elite Publications, Lead Pastor of Greater Vision Christian Church, an International Best-selling Author, Spiritual Empowerment Coach, and Blog Radio Host. She is a retired teacher for the Edgecombe County Public Schools System and the wife of Dr. Jessie Bowen. She has a weekly program featured on the GPAT-23 television station and hosts It's a GREATER Day every Tuesday and Thursday on Facebook Live.

Her books include *My Soul Cries Out; 30 Days Me & God: Daily Devotionals to Renew Your Mind; Don't Give Up in Your Storm: God is in Control in the Storms of Your Life;* and *I Choose to be the Greater Me: Living Life in Greatness.*

For more information, visit www.MinisterGwenBowen.com

CHAPTER 4

FEARFULLY & WONDERFULLY MADE

BY JESSICA CAROL-LYN

My Story

I remember being a happy young child and feeling my parents' love. However, I still felt a void that caused me to have identity issues. I wanted to be prettier and slimmer and live the glamorous life I saw on television. I wished for different features because my peers repeatedly teased me for the ones I had. Needless to say, I walked with my head down to avoid eye contact with anyone outside my family or friends.

Reflecting on this small glimpse into my childhood, it's clear that I didn't see myself as God did; instead, I related more to how others saw and labeled me. I could not see God extending His hand to me for a deeper relationship beyond the emptiness. I did not trust Him enough with my emotions and low self-esteem. Honestly, at that time, I did not realize that He cared so deeply about me and every issue that flowed from my heart. Unfortunately, I did not feel like I could talk to anyone about this, so I lived more than half my life comparing myself to others, desiring the "beauty" the world offers rather than accepting that I was created in the Creator's image.

That is until Jesus met me where I was, and I decided to have a relationship with Him and get to know Him for myself.

In my adulthood, my relationship with the Father developed during a difficult season when I was overwhelmed and exhausted with life. I had reached a point where I felt like I couldn't catch a break, and everything seemed to be hitting me hard. I was depressed, lonely, suicidal, grieving the loss of my mother and grandmother, emotionally unstable, heartbroken, spiritually weak, and on the verge of breaking down. With all this heartache and brokenness, I knew it was the right time to pray a desperate prayer, asking the Lord not to let me wake up the next day. I was indeed done with life and just wanted it to end. That night, I went through my usual routine, went to bed, and fully expected not to wake up on earth. But as you can see, that prayer I said over ten years ago was unanswered.

I'm grateful that God had other plans for me and loved me enough not to give me what I asked for. What He did next was even better. Although it was tough, it ultimately worked for my good and deepened my relationship with Him.

God shifted my entire world and rearranged my life. He removed me from a life that lacked Christ and the abundance He freely offered. This shift removed the lies of the enemy and people. I desired the Holy Spirit more than anything in this world; He became the air I breathed. I pursued the Lord with all my heart and began spending more time with Him. I was like a deer panting for water, as described in Psalm 42:1. I needed Him desperately, and the more I sought Him, the more I learned about Him. As I learned more about Him, I began to know Him. The more I knew Him, the more I began to know myself. I discovered who Jessica was without the labels others or I had placed on me. I fell in love with the image in the mirror because I had fallen in love with the Creator. I saw His heart for me, which spoke louder than any hurtful comment that had ever broken me and louder than the desperate prayer to end my life.

You're God's Masterpiece

If we take a look at Psalm 139:14, we will find that this verse includes praise from David to God because He made David (and us) so uniquely. Think about it: our features, fingerprints, personalities, and bodies are all uniquely created and are what make us individuals. David celebrated the fact that God created him by praising Him. Yes, he praised God. How often do we take the opportunity to praise God for making us how He did? How often do we admire (humbly) His work as it stares back at us in the mirror? How often do we thank Him for the nose, frame, hands, personality, freckles, and even the voice we have? I hate to say it, but it does not happen often. Instead of praising God for our individuality, we complain that we are too fat, skinny, short, tall, dark, or pale. Our forehead is too big, our nose is too large, our eyes are too far apart, and our hair is too curly or straight. These negative thoughts can lead to loneliness and feeling inadequate and unworthy to do His work, giving the enemy a chance to use these feelings to keep you stuck. But God wants you to be free.

Did you know the original Mona Lisa painting by Leonardo da Vinci is worth over US$800 million? Yet, if you went to an online store, you could purchase a replica of this great painting for as little as US$10. Do you see the vast difference in pricing? The original painting by the master artist, which took him years to complete, costs more because the painting passed through the inspection of the creator. He took his time selecting colors, textures, emotions, shadows, and other techniques before putting his signature on the completed piece of art.

You have gone through the same process. Psalm 139:13 says that God "created your inner body and knit you together in your mother's womb." If you know anything about knitting, it takes patience, practice, and skill. Everyone cannot knit. In fact, if you gave me needles, yarn, and a pattern, I would not have the ability to produce a perfect piece. But if you put the same needles and yarn in the hands of a skilled knitter, they would produce something exquisite.

Where am I going with this? You are valuable because the most suitable and skilled Creator made you just the way you are. You are wonderfully made, loved, and needed. When God created you, His plans and thoughts were (and still are) great towards you. Do not allow the words of others, your past, or your doubts to cheapen the value that God placed on you. Jesus loves you so much that He thought you were to die for (1 John 4:9–10).

Overcoming the Comparison Trap

"We do not dare to classify or compare ourselves with some who commend themselves. When they measure themselves by themselves and compare themselves with themselves, they are not wise." - 2 Corinthians 10:12 (NIV)

In today's digital age, comparison is just a swipe or click away. Social media platforms can become breeding grounds for insecurity and self-doubt. But when we fall into the comparison trap, we're essentially telling God that His design isn't good enough.

Remember this: Your journey is unique. The path God has laid out for you is tailored specifically to your growth, purpose, and relationship with Him. Comparing your behind-the-scenes struggles to someone else's highlight reel is unfair and detrimental to your spiritual and emotional well-being.

Reflection Exercise #1:

1. Conduct a social media audit. Unfollow or mute accounts that consistently make you feel inadequate or trigger unhealthy comparisons.
2. Start a gratitude journal, focusing on the unique qualities and blessings God has given you.
3. When tempted to compare, redirect your thoughts to God's love and purpose for your life.

Discovering Your God-Given Purpose

"For I know the plans I have for you," declares the LORD, "plans to prosper you and not to harm you, plans to give you hope and a future." - Jeremiah 29:11 (NIV)

Loving who God created you to be goes hand in hand with understanding your divine purpose. You are not a cosmic accident or a random assemblage of cells. You were created with the intention of a specific mission that only you can fulfill.

Your purpose isn't necessarily tied to a particular career or achievement. It's about reflecting God's love, using your unique gifts to serve others, and growing in your relationship with Him. Sometimes, our purpose unfolds gradually, like a flower slowly blooming. Other times, it may become clear in a moment of divine revelation.

Reflection Exercise #2:

1. What activities make you lose track of time?
2. When do you feel most alive and connected to God?
3. How can your struggles and experiences be used to help others?

These questions can provide clues to your God-given purpose. As you explore them, remain open to God's guidance and be patient with the process.

Embracing Your Spiritual Identity

"See what great love the Father has lavished on us, that we should be called children of God! And that is what we are!" - 1 John 3:1 (NIV)

At the core of loving who God created you to be is embracing your spiritual identity as a child of God. This identity transcends your earthly roles, accomplishments, or shortcomings. It's an unshakeable foundation rooted in God's unconditional love.

When you fully grasp your identity in Christ, it transforms how you view yourself and navigate life's challenges:

- *You are loved* unconditionally (Romans 8:38-39)

- *You are forgiven* completely (Ephesians 1:7)
- *You are accepted* wholly (Ephesians 1:6)
- *You are valuable* beyond measure (Matthew 10:29-31)
- *You are empowered* by the Holy Spirit (Acts 1:8)

Embracing these truths doesn't mean you'll never struggle with self-doubt or insecurity. But it provides a solid foundation to return to when negative thoughts creep in.

Practical Application: Create visual reminders of your identity in Christ. This could be scripture cards placed around your home, a customized phone wallpaper, or a piece of jewelry that symbolizes your worth in God's eyes.

Cultivating Self-Love Through God's Eyes

How might your relationships and ministry be impacted if you fully embraced and loved who God created you to be? Loving who God created you to be isn't about narcissism or self-obsession. It's about honoring God by cherishing His creation – you. When we view ourselves through God's eyes, we develop a healthy, balanced self-love that empowers us to love others more fully.

Here are some practical ways to cultivate this God-centered self-love:

1. **Practice self-compassion**: Treat yourself with the same kindness and understanding you would offer a dear friend.

2. **Celebrate your progress**: Acknowledge your growth, no matter how small. Every small step forward leads to a big victory.
3. **Speak life**: Pay attention to your self-talk. Replace negative, critical thoughts with affirming, biblical truths.
4. **Care for your whole self**: Honor God by taking care of your physical, emotional, and spiritual health.
5. **Embrace your story**: Your experiences – both triumphs and trials – have shaped you. Trust that God can use every part of your journey for His glory.

As we conclude this chapter, remember that loving who God created you to be is a journey, not a destination. There will be days when it feels more manageable and days when it's more of a struggle. But in every moment, God's love for you remains constant and unwavering.

You are seen. You are known. You are loved beyond measure.

Embrace the beautiful, unique individual God created you to be, and watch how it transforms your life and those around you.

A Prayer for Embracing Your God-Given Identity

Heavenly Father,

Thank you for creating me with purpose and love. Forgive me for the times I've doubted Your design or wished to be someone else. Help me to see myself through Your eyes – as a masterpiece, fearfully and wonderfully made.

Lord, I pray for the courage to embrace my unique qualities and the wisdom to use them for Your glory. Guard my heart against unhealthy comparisons, and help me find my worth in You alone.

Guide me as I discover and live out the purpose You've set for my life. May I always remember that I am Your beloved child, fully loved, accepted, and empowered by Your Spirit.

Thank you for the gift of being me. Help me to love and cherish who You created me to be so that I might reflect Your love to the world around me.

In Jesus' name, *Amen.*

Reflection Exercise #3:

1. What is one aspect of yourself that you struggle to love? How might God view this characteristic?
2. How has comparing yourself to people affected your relationship with God and others?
3. What steps can you take this week to practically embrace and celebrate your God-given identity?

Daily Affirmation:

I am more than enough.

I am destined for greatness.

I am fearfully and wonderfully made.

I am God's masterpiece.

Jessica Carol-lyn

Remember: I am rooting for you!

JESSICA CAROL-LYN
DEVOTIONAL

$\mathcal{W\!E}$ LOOK TO GOD

"Yet no one calls on your name or pleads with you for mercy. Therefore, you have turned away from us and turned us over to our sins. And yet, O Lord, you are our Father. We are the clay, and you are the potter. We all are formed by your hand." (Isaiah 64:7-8)

To be fearfully and wonderfully made means we look to God, not everyone else. Fortunately, God made a way for us to repent and turn to Him by sending His very own Son to make the way. When you realize that without God, you are unable to make the most of yourself, that's when things begin to change. The clay cannot mold itself, no matter how hard it tries. However, God, the Potter, cannot only mold His clay, but He also knows what His original design of you was. He is both a Potter and an Architect with a master plan.

Sometimes, in this fallen world, people are born with birth defects that disrupt one or more of the intricate systems of the body. God foresaw even those defects and uses them for good when we look to Him. Even our weaknesses are fearfully and wonderfully made.

A blind person can develop hearing beyond the normal capacity. Conjoined twins can teach us about getting along with one another, for they have to do it 24/7. Someone born without arms develops the ability to use their feet in wondrous ways. Another born without legs develops the upper body strength to get around smoothly.

We all have weaknesses that sometimes make us feel like we are of no use. But God's grace is sufficient to cover our weaknesses. More than that, God's power is made perfect in our weaknesses. Weaknesses keep us humble and leaning on God's strength, which is much more sufficient than my own.

Prayer:

Dear Lord, Thank You for how fearfully and wonderfully You've created me. Thank You for always seeing the goodness in me. May I purposefully live the life you have ordained. In Jesus' Name, *Amen.*

ABOUT
*J*ESSICA CAROL-LYN

Jessica Carol-lyn is a Christian Minister, Youth Mentor, Martial Artist, Award-winning Author, and Magazine Columnist. Her books include *Be D.O.P.E.: Be Dependent on Prayer Every Day, Volumes I & II*, which help readers develop a deeper relationship with Christ. Jessica says, "There's something about how my pen flows when God writes through me. I'm in love with His words and penmanship."

Jessica has also co-authored numerous international best-selling books, including *The Art of Connection and Elite Black Belts Who Cook.* Her academic achievements include being inducted into prestigious honor societies such as Phi Theta Kappa and the National Society of Leadership and Success. In 2022, Jessica received the Presidential Community Service Lifetime Achievement Award, signed by President Joe Biden.

Jessica believes in the power of her words and only speaks greatness into her life and the lives of others. Additionally, she believes that she is not only capable of reaching for the stars, but through Christ, she can touch them, too. By sharing Jesus, her experiences, and insights, she hopes to inspire others to do the same.

For more information, please visit:
bit.ly/JessicaCarollynAuthor

$\mathcal{S}$TAY FOCUSED.
SEEK HIM $\mathcal{E}$ KNOW HIM

BY EVANGELIST ANNIE HOWARD

Sitting at the foot of my bed, I began to think of the goodness of God and how He has kept me. Oh, what a blessing it is "To Know Him." As thoughts revisited me, I remembered when I was a little girl and my getting hit by a car and left paralyzed; I was diagnosed twice with cancer; how I went blind while attending service in the church, and God restored my sight. At that moment, I could hear the words of David so clearly being spoken from Psalm 23: The LORD is my shepherd; I shall not want. He maketh me to lie down in green pastures: he leadeth me beside the still waters. He restoreth my soul: he leadeth me in the paths of righteousness for his names sake. Yea, though I walk through the valley of the shadow of death, I will fear no evil: for thou art with me; thy rod and thy staff they comfort me.

Thou preparest a table before me in the presence of mine enemies: thou anointest my head with oil; my cup runneth over. Surely goodness and mercy shall follow me all the days of my life: and I will dwell in the house of the LORD forever.

I am so grateful to God. I have endured a lot in my life, but He has always restored my soul through it all. He has always been there to guide me, feed me with more knowledge of who He is, and provide me with a hedge of protection. I know what it means "to walk through the valley of the shadow of death," but I also learned during those valley experiences, He was always with me, and I had nothing to fear.

In 2018, my husband, George, went home to be with the Lord. Oh, the loneliness I felt. We were blessed to share 40 years together as husband and wife. He shared his life not only with me but also with his pet dog, Buster. Shortly after he passed, Buster passed away, and if that was not enough, the goldfish passed away. I felt so alone. I've learned that your life seasons bring about changes you never thought you would encounter. We find we have to refocus. In doing so, we have to make what some would seem like drastic decisions. That was where I found myself. I had to sell my house and return my car to the car dealership. I no longer had those things that I had considered mine, but I was thankful He had allowed me to keep my mind.

God let me know that during those times, you have to stay focused. You have to keep your eyes and your mind focused on where you're going and what you're going to do because the things and the cares of this world will tie you down. They will tie your mind down, but if you've focused on Jesus, know where you are going, and know that nothing else matters, you can make it.

You know, you think about Job and how Job lost everything. His wife wanted him to curse God and die. See, that's what the enemy will say. Don't you see how we are going through so much, and Satan wants us to give up? Throw our hands up. But, you know what, I'm looking forward. I'm moving on. Even as a wife, I learned to be that good wife. And no, it wasn't all easy days. Some days were up, and some days were down. But you know what I did? I learned to stay focused. Sometimes, women, we go through something, but you've got to keep your mind and remain on Jesus. He does not want us to be weak women, but he wants us to be strong women. Sometimes when you feel like you can't take anymore - the children, your job, and even if you are a pastor, it becomes too much; you've got to know that sometimes you need to take a break. Sometimes you need to hide yourself in that secret place with Him. Sometimes, you need to get away by yourself. Go to the beauty shop and get your nails done, or you might want to go to a nice restaurant and sit there alone. Sometimes, you've got to shut yourself down. We have to take care of ourselves, and then we have to know who we are. If you don't love yourself, how can anybody else love you? No matter how people look or see you, you've got to know who you are, and you have to keep yourself beautified on the inside, not just the outside.

We are beautiful; we are queens. We have to know who we are and who we are in Christ. How can we expect other people to know if we don't know that? Take care of yourself. Dress yourself respectfully when you go out. Don't go out looking anyway. Although you are not out there to please people, you know who you represent.

Those who are married, you got to love your husband. Ask God to allow the Holy Spirit to teach you how to love your husband. Let him know he is your king and the king of the house. Respect him, and he will respect you. Some of you wonder why he's looking at another woman; it's because she makes sure she respects herself and knows how to talk to him. Refocus! Dress yourself in your cute outfit, welcome him home, fix him a homecooked meal, stop going to KFC all the time, and clean the house.

I want to tell you women, even single women. I want to say this to you. You are blessed. You can't go out and hang out with your friends. You can't do all of those things you did as a single woman because you now have taken on the responsibility of being a wife and loving your husband. And yes, it's a two-way street. You have to show him love, and he shows you love.

Jesus said He would never leave us, neither would He forsake us. We are powerful women. Look at the women in the Bible. They were with Jesus. They were the first to tell the good news that Jesus was alive. We are women with power. We have to use our power to pull down the strongholds. When we see the enemy attacking your husband and your children, know that he has given us power, then know – that no weapon formed against you shall prosper (Isiah 54.17).

I was married for 40 years. I can tell you something. Did I say it was all good? No, it wasn't all good, but neither was it bad. When I got married, I would say my husband and I were out there in the world together. I had to make that first step. I got tired. I know what it is to be abused. When I got saved, I shared Jesus with him. I knew I couldn't live like that anymore. I wanted to change, and he did, too. I want to tell you the good thing about change. You let go of the bad and focus on the good. I remember when I met my husband. I was sitting on the picnic table, and when he came by, he said, "You want to be my lady?" I was his lady for 40 years.

By the grace of God, we stuck by each other until the day he took his last breath. I'll never forget when we went behind Phillipi Church and dedicated our lives to God together. He will always be in my heart.

Women, I am a witness; you don't know how blessed you are until you lose a spouse. When he goes home with the

Lord, it's a different feeling that stays in your heart. Even if you decide to marry again, you can't expect that man to be what your previous husband was because it's a whole different relationship. So, I want to encourage you to stay focused, stay in your lane, and know that you are beautiful, and nobody or nothing can change that because you know who you are.

Men, the Bible says in Proverbs 18:22, "He who finds a wife finds a good thing and obtaineth favour of the Lord." You need to know that one of the best things about being in a marriage is knowing your partner has your back through the ups and downs life will inevitably bring. When it comes to having a wife, men have said there is nothing better than the knowledge and trust that comes when they know their wives support them.

God didn't create Eve to be under Adam's feet or to be inferior to him. When the design of marriage became a construction zone, God saw it fit to create a sister joist. Eve was designed and built to support Adam. This was the construction and structure of the first marriage.

"And the Lord God said, 'It is not good that man should be alone; I will make him a helper comparable to him'" (Gen. 2:18). The word helper means one who aids another. Thus, the woman was created because the man needed help from someone who could aid him in his responsibilities. Take note that Eve was created to be comparable to Adam. The word comparable means one who is a counterpart or the matching mate of the other.

A house is just a house until the use of your talents, soul, personality, and nurturing make it a home. It's been said that a wife is the heart of the home. That's because wives meet their husband's and children's needs.

Men, you have also been given a great responsibility. You have to think of your wife as your queen. And as your queen, you must ensure she is alright, always being there to care for her. You have to shower her with the fruit of the Spirit: love, joy, peace, forbearance, kindness, goodness, faithfulness, gentleness, and self-control (Galatians 5:22-23). Learn to communicate together. I'm talking about a real man and the king of his own house. Know when it's time to go on vacation, not needing a reason to take her to dinner or shower her with flowers, and not just on Valentine's Day or her birthday, but always showing her that you care.

In any relationship, communication is number one. Even before bed, always sit down and ensure everything is alright. Talk about your day and your expectations for tomorrow. Whatever needs to be worked on, work on it together before it gets out of hand. I'm talking about a real man and his queen. Together, they walk out of the past and walk into the future with God as their guide.

I learned in sharing 40 years of marriage with my husband that you have to know Him. You have to know God. God will keep your marriage, strengthen your marriage, and even beautify your marriage — as you each focus most on seeking Him.

"Seek first the kingdom of God and his righteousness," *Jesus says, "and all these things will be added to you"* *(Matthew 6:33).*

EVANGELIST ANNIE HOWARD
DEVOTIONAL

O NOT DWELL

"Then, I saw a new Heaven and a new Earth, for the first Heaven and the first Earth had passed away, and there was no longer any sea." (Revelation 21:1)

I am making a new Heaven and a new Earth. I am preparing my people - all around the world - to live there with Me in endless ecstasy. Let this eternal perspective strengthen and encourage you.

Forget the former things; do not dwell on the past. As you journey along your life path with Jesus, refuse to let the past define you or your expectations of what lies ahead. You may feel as if the road you are on is tiresome or even a dead end. That is because you're projecting the past into the future. The future is in His hands, and He can do surprising things with it!

Your greatest danger is giving up: ceasing to believe Jesus can still do wondrous new things in you and your world. Your assignment is to keep moving forward and trust and depend on Him. Stop focusing on obstacles you might encounter and concentrate on staying in touch with Him. As you continue taking steps of trust, expect the path before you to open up in refreshing newness.

Prayer:

Lord, thank You for who I am in You. I will not allow my past to define my future. I am trusting and believing that You will do new and wonderous things in my life. I will focus on the present, for there I will find YOU. *Amen*

ABOUT
ANNIE HOWARD

Evangelist Annie Spencer Howard is truly a woman of God. She has been pastoring and preaching the gospel for over 40 years, hosted a radio show, Power of Prayer, for 20 years, and presently shares virtually on Facebook Live Keep It Real and Pray to empower God's children.

She was married to the late George Howard for 40 years. Evangelist Howard knows the Word, professes the Word, will speak the Word into your life, and will preach the Word. She has encountered many visitations from angels, and they always bring a message to her from God, whether showing her or telling her what God is saying so that she can tell His people.

She is the author of *Spiritual Visions: My Daily Walk with Jesus: God's Messenger.*

CHAPTER 6

CALLED TO KNOW GOD & TO MAKE HIM KNOWN

BY DR. SOPHONY LAMOUR

Our experiences help shape our understanding of the true and living God. These experiences, whether joyful or challenging, serve as invitations to know God intimately.

My experiences with God, which I share partly, demonstrate the transformative power of knowing God in his divinity and sovereignty. He displays himself as the healer, the defender, the protector, the God of love, and the profound significance of His presence in my life, as He seeks to be in all of our lives.

Understanding the significance of knowing God and making Him known through life experiences is crucial. I refer to "knowing" as the knowledge that initiates change, a quest, and yields results.

My walk with God began at an early age. At one year old, I was left with my grandmother while my mother traveled to pursue the American dream. This dream led me to believe that the sky is the limit within the socio-economic sphere, promising great joy, adventure, and excitement.

As I desired to meet and be with my mother, it was an experience that left me now understanding how God sought His very own relationship with me through my experiences. My encounter with God began growing up in church at the age of eight.

One day, as I stood on the rooftop of the house, I expressed my desire to know my mother silently in a heartfelt outpouring of my heart. I never uttered a word, but I expressed it in my heart as I looked up and enjoyed the sky, believing that God was up there in the sky; He heard me. This leads me to understand that God waits for our understanding to develop enough to connect with His existence. Connection is a compelling thing. Knowing and connecting with that knowledge is what makes things happen. Humanity's longing to know is sometimes where divine intervention patiently waits for our petitions to God, who awaits to fulfill our requests.

God is so transcendent that He announces the end from the beginning. One of my favorite scriptures is Isaiah 65:24;

listen to what the Lord Himself tells us about prayer: "It will come to pass that before they call, I will answer; and while they are still speaking, I will hear." The answer to our prayers is prepared before we pray. The desire to talk to the Lord about our needs comes from Him. However, we must be in the posture to respond and engage with God by choosing to connect sincerely with Him. My very first encounter with God, with sincerity in my heart, taught me powerful lessons: that God hears the whispers of my heart and the unspoken cries of His children, responding with swift and tender grace.

Through divine intervention, He orchestrated a miraculous turn of events, guiding my path and reuniting me with my mom while demonstrating His divine power and provision in doing so. What am I saying? Your experiences with God are never as simple as they seem. They teach lessons you will need to walk with Him for your journey. Sometimes, one can wonder about the relationship and the power it holds. It is also possible to not be aware of the power within your relationships. One of the powers of a relationship is simply "to know." To know someone, to be acquainted with them, to be very familiar with them are not often things we contemplate. "To know" is further defined as being aware of through observation, inquiry, or information. It means to be confident or sure about something.

As I matured and had so many experiences with God in my walk with Him, from psycho-socio challenges to financial, marital, health, etc., the core of the relationship with God is to know Him. It is in knowing Him that all puzzles are solved, all mysteries provide answers, and everything that is out of alignment finds its alignment. Knowing Him brings resolutions and answers to queries.

I have consistently seen the manifestation of God in my daily life, living in the United States of America and my international travels. Allow me to pose an investigative and provocative thought: *When did you first realize that God is real in your life?* In addition to the grave, severe, life-threatening, some impossibilities and even the threat of homicide, suicide, and ravaging cancers that later presented themselves, this very first encounter I had with God taught me I couldn't ever convince myself even if I wanted to, that God is not real to me.

The "knowing," the "seeking," and the "relationship" are connectivity that demonstrates God's sovereignty, power, divinity, and relatability. Some say they seek God through prayer and do not see God's hand. Yet, God gives us a blueprint in several ways: "You will seek me and find me, when you seek me with all your heart," Jeremiah 29:13.

In any relationship of interests, we take time to know a person of interest, someone who intrigues us, someone we admire or seek to emulate. Take a short journey with me and see where my relationship with God through Christ Jesus makes a difference. My need for a miracle, my need for the prayer-answering God, and most of all, my need for a relationship with God determine whether His presence in my life is a place of dwelling or a place of visitation.

In seeking to know and learn about God, I realized that He speaks back to me. We often use terms such as "virtuous woman," typically referring to a woman of admirable qualities, encompassing a range of positive traits, such as strength. At a point in my life, I became very uncomfortable being called a woman of great strength. It made me nervous to be referred to as such.

To have developed and to develop such characteristics means to go through testing. I had gone through so many complex and challenging experiences that I did not want to go through them anymore. I was concerned that such strength could attract further testing. Before gold can be purified, it must go through the highest level of fire. Manufacturers test their products for resilience and knowledge of outcomes.

Similarly, to know God requires a level of intimacy that has been tested with continual upgrades. Giving birth to my first-born baby, the dilemmas that arose during the pregnancy stage and beyond were unfathomable. After my first year of marriage, I was met with a monthly menstrual cycle of heavy flow and blood clots while becoming anemic.

Having visited with my doctor, he decided to provide a solution to regulate the heavy flow of the menstrual cycle by giving birth control pills. At the time, I had no idea I was pregnant, nor did the doctor conduct a pregnancy test. Psychologically, as a teenager, I was always too scared to swallow pills and could never swallow a pill. Consequently, I never even tried to drink one.

This leaves me to believe that God sends us with some built-in protective mechanism within our own selves that serves as a shield in some areas of our lives. The God who sees all and who knows all. He is so much God that he announces the end from the beginning. Had I taken that pill, my daughter would have died.

There are things we do not understand, but the psalmist said we will understand it better by and by. My first-born daughter is truly a miracle baby; from birth, her life was threatened. During birth, a lack of oxygen went to her brain. She was born asphyxiated, with a lack of oxygen reaching her brain, born blue, and had to be resuscitated.

She was later diagnosed with speech delay, mental retardation, and multiple handicaps. She could not walk. Fast forward to the age of seven, she was met with a fast-growing cancerous brain tumor the size of a watermelon. It took prayer to heal her and sustain her. The surgeon said she took every piece of the mass out of her brain. While the surgeon recommended chemotherapy, she did not recommend radiotherapy and said radiotherapy could create more cancer and cause it to spread throughout her body. Before being discharged from the hospital after the surgery, a doctor came to see me, asking if I wanted to have my daughter participate in a trial. And, said, since my daughter does not need it, I should think about how many children's lives my daughter can save by participating in this medical trial.

Two months passed, and my husband, a Pastor, was at church teaching bible study. I received a phone call in the early afternoon from the hospital's social worker who said, "Mrs. St. Cloud, I am so sorry to have to call you to tell you that the doctor who asked for your daughter to be a participant in his trial is making me do this. He has asked me to call ACS (Administration for Children Services) on you, Mrs. St. Cloud, and I am so sorry." Then, a court battle ensued right before the Christmas holiday. I was charged with medical negligence.

The oncologist tried to use the internal sutures from the surgery to claim that the cancer had returned due to not participating in his medical trial. God's Word says, "No weapon formed against us will prosper, and every tongue that rises up against us is silent!!!" Weapons can form, but they will not prosper!!! God's demonstrated healing power is evident.

Knowing God and trusting His omnipotence are crucial. In the natural, the doctor had requested daily radiation therapy; I took my daughter to God's house for prayer daily, laying her down at the altar in the presence of God. Less than a year later, my last-born child, my only son, was diagnosed with the same cancer in the exact location.

But this time, because he was four years old at the time, doctors said he needed to have a shunt (a small tube) that tunnels from his brain down to his abdomen because his body is unable to have the brain fluid form on its own. Again, God showed his incredible power and love and healed him. Doctors said that he would need to have surgery yearly to replace the shunt inside his brain.

It has been 29 years.; he has never been under the knife, and the shunt has never been changed. One year, upon completing an annual x-ray, the doctor panicked. The X-ray showed that the shunt had broken. I told the doctor my son was fine; I said my son was better than us.

The broken shunt did not threaten his life and did not make him sick. He was not showing any of the expected symptoms for a nonfunctioning shunt. Jesus has the last say. When he heals, the healing is final. He heals outside of medicine, and he can heal with medicine. He is the great I am that I am.

The power of knowing God, trusting in God, and relying on Him through relationship in Christ Jesus is power and authority through Him and in Him. A few years later, I was then diagnosed with breast cancer and was asked to take a pill for five years for preventive measures. I had a mastectomy. I trusted God and prayed for God's divine healing. And I was healed.

As I exercised faith in God, trusting and relying on Him, I have learned that nothing can replace a true relationship with Him. Our faith will be tested, but our faith in God is what causes us to overcome by the words of our testimonies. We are called to know God for ourselves. Only then can we share what we have with others.

Sometimes, our faith must testify that we can believe God for ourselves as much as we can believe God to move for others. In my recent mission trip to Pakistan, preaching the gospel of Jesus Christ, many souls stood up to be saved and healed. How can we be a testament to his miraculous work if we do not yield to Him in prayer with trust and reliance that He is who He says He is and He will do what He says He will do through those who take the time to know Him and to make Him known through our personal experiences.

God says that it will come to pass that he has already answered before His children call Him, and while His children continue to speak, He hears (Isaiah 65:24). We have all been called to a purposeful life, and our life experiences are part of our journey. Our experiences are the hope of the calling to know God. As we share our stories and experiences, we make known his divinity and the hope of glory. *Knowing Him is a relationship. Making Him known is a relationship demonstrated with power within our purposeful journey.*

In conclusion, our journey of faith with life experiences serves as a light toward a more profound knowledge of God. Each experience becomes a testament to His divinity and the transformative power of His love. Sharing these stories strengthens our relationship with God and serves as a path for others to discover His power, divinity, love, grace, and mercy. Therefore, let us embrace our calling to know God intimately and to make Him known through the power of our testimonies. For in doing so, we not only fulfill our purpose but also shine brightly as reflections of His glory in a world *called to know His love.*

DR. SOPHONY LAMOUR
DEVOTIONAL

AMILY

"Love is patient, love is kind. It does not envy, it does not boast, it is not proud. It does not dishonor others, it is not self-seeking, it is not easily angered, it keeps no record of wrongs. Love does not delight in evil but rejoices with the truth. It always protects, always trusts, always hopes, always perseveres. Love never fails." (1 Corinthians 13:4-8)

As you live your life of faith before your family, it's like stocking a vault that will bless everyone. And it's never too late to begin. As you live before God, leave a blueprint for those who are watching. That example can last for generations, beyond your view, more influential than you can imagine. Your influence on your family is phenomenal - for good and for bad. Sadly, some of us weaken our families through selfishness, ambition, and carelessness. The vigilant, wise, and godly parent holds their family together, makes sacrifices to ensure its stability, and entreats God's blessing with their prayers. You can be that kind of parent - the kind that builds up and strengthens. Ask God to help you. He will show you how.

Prayer:

Dear God,

Help me to be a phenomenal parent. That parent who lives a life for You that I might inspire someone else to be all that they might be in You. Help me, show me, bless me. *Amen*

ABOUT
$\mathscr{S}$OPHONY LAMOUR

Dr. Sophony Lamour is a passionate advocate whose influence extends beyond church walls. Her name, "Sophonie," from Zephaniah, meaning "the one whom the Lord has rescued," reflects her life of overcoming challenges through divine intervention. Her testimony of God's healing and deliverance is profoundly inspiring.

Dedicated to living for Jesus and guided by the Holy Spirit, Dr. Lamour serves as the International President of Missions with the Kingdom Impact Movement (KIM) and The Stanley Gorrell Ministries (SGM). She serves under her father, Apostle Archbishop Stanley Gorrell, focusing on spiritual and economic support for disadvantaged communities and collaborating with global leaders to improve lives.

With over twenty years as an Evangelist and ten years as Co-Pastor of Holy Spirit Revival, Dr. Lamour served under the late Bishop Norman N. Quick. Additionally, she worked with the Women's Division of the General Board of Global Ministries, The United Methodist Church, at the United Nations (UN) on global affairs, immigrant, civil, and human rights, and global, economic, and environmental justice. She liaised with UN agencies, heads of state, diplomats, ecumenical ecclesiastical leaders, and inter-faith leaders within the UN Community.

A graduate of Seton Hall University School of Law with a Jurisprudence and Health Law degree, Dr. Lamour also holds a Doctor of Divinity and is pursuing a Doctor of Theology. She leads Hidden Halos Kingdom Assets, which is dedicated to fulfilling God's call for kingdom building and sustaining others in their divine destiny.

For more information, please visit www.hiddenhalos-kingdomassets.com

Facebook: @hiddenhaloskingdomasset

Instagram: @hidden_halos_kingdom_assets

YouTube Channel: @hiddenhaloskingdomassets7087

LinkedIn: linkedin.com/company/hidden-halos-kingdom-assets-inc

CHAPTER 7

OH, HOW COULD I FORGET?

BY ANNIE WATTS

Dedication

In honor of my deceased grandmothers, Ethel Harris and
Lottie Nicholson, and my mom, Mamie Nicholson, who first
introduced me to the teachings of Christ and the sweet
fellowship with like believers. My mother, Mamie
Nicholson, taught me how to live by The Golden Rule: Treat
others as you would like others to treat you, leave things
better than you found them, and pray as Jesus taught His
disciples, but in your unique ways. I thank you for nurturing
me with love and instilling good ethics that make me the
person that I am today; oh, How Could I Forget!

The Lord's Prayer:

Our Father, who art in heaven, Hallowed be Thy name. Thy
kingdom come, Thy will be done in earth, as it is in heaven.

Give us this day our daily bread. And forgive us our debts as we forgive our debtors. And lead us not into temptation, but deliver us from evil: For Thine is the kingdom, and the power, and the glory, forever. *Amen.*

"But Jesus said, suffer little children, and forbid them not, to come unto me: for of such, is the kingdom of heaven." (Matthew 19:14)

Acknowledgments

As I have been taught to edify God, I glorify and praise Him for being a constant guiding Light in my life. Also, I want to thank God for blessing me with a village of spiritual advisors who pray for me. To my readers, I pray that God continues to guide you as you travel on your Christian journey. With great respect and honor, I acknowledge Dr. Gwendolyn Bowen for inviting me to co-author this book. I have always dreamed of becoming an author. Today, I thank God for blessing me with this privilege and for my devoted friend. Today, I humbly share my dream of authorship and memorable inspirations with my family and friends. I pray your faith continues to grow each day and that you find fulfillment in your endeavors. When challenges come, I'm comforted by the words of the song, "Peace be Still." I find peace and happiness in knowing that he controls my future. I pray that you find your guiding light. He is worthy of being praised! To God be the Glory for what He has done for me. Oh, How Could I Forget? Amen and Amen!

"The LORD hath appeared of old unto me, saying, Yea, I have loved thee with an everlasting love: therefore, with lovingkindness have I drawn thee." (Jeremiah 31:3)

As a young child and even now, two of my favorite praise and worship songs are "We've Come This Far by Faith" and "It's Another Day's Journey." I remember visiting my Grandmother Harris' church on special occasions. I enjoyed listening to the Oakey Grove Missionary Baptist Church's senior choir sing their hearts out as the piano player made the black and white keys keep the beat. Their performance was always wonderful. My siblings and I enjoyed watching our grandmother spring from her pew into her unique holy dance. We knew we were in church, but we sure did get a kick out of watching her move like that. As we became rowdy, clapping our hands and keeping up with the beat of the music, the other church mothers would lay their eyes on us. We knew what that look meant. Some things you pray that you'll never forget; for me, it is spending time with my mom and grandmothers.

Grandmother Harris always made sure that I participated in the Children's Day Program by reciting a poem or saying a Bible verse. As time moved on, my grandmother took piano lessons and purchased a big piano. After learning how to play the piano, she would sing and play a melody of traditional hymns for all her guests. Her love was steadfast, and because of that, she often prayed, sang songs, and spoke encouraging words for us to live by. My grandmother was a very proud God-fearing woman who taught us to say thank you, to pray, and to thank God for our daily bread, family, life, health, and strength.

"But seek first his kingdom and his righteousness, and all these things will be given to you as well." (Mathew 6:33)

I remember when my mom started buying Bible storybooks from traveling booksellers. I loved looking at the biblical pictures because I could understand the text and relate to Sunday morning sermons. You know they say a picture is worth a thousand words, and that was very true for us. Early on, two of my favorite childhood stories were about Noah's Ark and the Crucifixion. Every Easter season, we would watch The Ten Commandments and The Crucifixion on television. I always loved watching those shows on television because they inspired me to want to know more about God. My mom started a family ritual. She read to us from our big family Bible, sang songs from an old hymnal, and helped us learn a new Bible verse that we had to recite during children's hour at church. My mom prayed for us and taught us how to pray for ourselves and others. She taught us a bedtime prayer, which we said nightly before getting into bed. Before retiring, we would get on bended knees, close our eyes, and say our prayer as Mother listened to us:

Now I lay me down to sleep,

I pray the Lord my soul to keep.

If I should die before I wake,

I pray the Lord my soul to take.

"Train up a child in the way he should go, and when he is old, he will not depart from it." (Proverbs 22:6)

My upbringing was modest, and sometimes, our blended families didn't have many things we needed, but we were thankful for what we had and each other. I've witnessed God making ways for us repeatedly. At the age of twelve, I felt the covenant of God shielding and protecting me, for He knew I would need His guidance. This is where I introduce you to my other praying grandma, Lottie Nicholson, known as Momma. She wasn't called Big Momma, but she was called Momma. Momma helped my mother and daddy take care of us. She, too, taught us about God's love, being respectable, and being obedient. She would tell us that obedience is better than sacrifice. We soon learned what she meant. She had a helper that grew on the ditch bank. When we got off course, we were instructed to go to the bush and bring back three switches, and they better be good ones, or there would be a consequence. Those three plaited switches helped Momma communicate her point, and we learned quickly.

On a different note, Momma had many talents. Momma always cooked the best fried chicken, hot biscuits, apple dumplings, and tea cakes. Not only was she a fantastic cook, but she was also a seamstress. She had one of those old-fashioned Singer sewing machines. I used to sit and watch her operate the machine by pressing the footpress to make the material slide under the needle. Together, Momma and my mother made our clothes out of cornmeal sacks. I guess you can say that Momma could do anything; she was our big Momma.

As time moved on, Momma started taking me to church with her. Those times were unforgettable because that's when my spiritual life began. I joined my grandmother Lottie's church and was baptized in a muddy creek in Vanceboro, NC; I felt a newness of joy from the Lord as the saints sang an old familiar hymn, *"Take me to the Water"* as the preacher dipped me in the water.

Over the years, I have had some ups and downs, but I have kept my faith through it all. My grandmother, Lottie Nicholson, always told me about the goodness of God and how He blesses and protects us from seen and unseen danger. I praise God for His forgiveness of our sins. I'm a born-again Christian who believes Christ gave His life for our sins, and if we live right, heaven belongs to us. I've had times when I was at my lowest point and didn't know which way to go. Thank God, my praying parents taught me to call upon the Lord. We are God's children; He hears our faithful cry and answers prayers when we call upon Him. I prayed and asked God to take control of my life. He gives me peace of mind, wraps his loving arms around me, renews my strength, and reminds me that I'm His child. He is worthy of being praised. *Hallelujah!*

"Jesus answered, Verily, verily, I say unto thee, except a man be born of water and Spirit, he cannot enter the kingdom of God." (John 3:5)

Sometimes, our plans are not meant to be because God has other plans for us. I believe that when He closes one door, He opens another one. As we evolve and navigate through our journey of life, we find that some of our circumstances, friends, and relationships grow and change. We often experience degrees of happiness, sorrow, disappointments, misunderstandings, successes, and even failures. We find ourselves celebrating or asking why. We are taught to praise God in and out of our season. I've had to pray to God to help me accept things that are not mine to change, especially when my mother and grandparents became my guardian angels. I praise God for the support of my family, my church family, Sycamore Hill Missionary Baptist Church, and my loving, supportive believers.

There is a saying from an old movie, *Who Are You Going To Call*, and I have another song that we use to sing, *"Jesus is on the main line; tell Him what you want."* Dearly beloved, we know there is a name above all others that we can call upon and put our trust in. So many titles reference Him. When I call upon Him, I say, God, my heavenly Father, and sometimes my Savior. He knows your heart, and He has a plan for your life. All you must do is confess your sins, ask for forgiveness, pray, give your life to Christ, and surround yourself with like believers.

We are blessed to have so many great spiritual resources at our fingertips. I have included a few references in my chapter just for you. In God, I hope you find guidance, peace, happiness, and fulfillment as you travel on your journey. As I stand on the shoulders of all those who prayed for me and inspired me, I pray that your warriors will do the same for you. May God continue to watch over us day by day. Oh, how could I forget the ones who taught me that our *God is our Everything?*

Many, Lord my God, are the wonders you have done, the things you planned for us. (Psalm 40:5)

God's Emergency Contact Numbers:

(Source: www.empowermissions.org)

1. Stressed - Matthew 11:25 – 30
2. Worried - Matthew 6:19 -34
3. Lonely - Psalm 23
4. Disappointed - Psalm 27
5. Bitter and Critical - 1 Corinthians 13
6. Sinned - Psalm 51
7. Discouraged - Psalm 34
8. Losing Hope - Psalm 139, Romans 8
9. Sick - Psalm 41, James 5:14
10. Sad - John 14
11. In Danger - Psalm 91
12. Scared - Isaiah 41:10, Joshua 1:9
13. Lacking Faith - Hebrews 11
14. Lacking Money - Psalm 37
15. Depressed - Psalm 27
16. Hurt - John 15
17. Treated Others Bad - Romans 12
18. Negative - Colossians 3:12 - 17, 1 Thessalonians 5:16 – 18

"Then you will call upon me and come and pray to me, and I will listen to you. You will seek me and find me when you seek me with your heart." (Jeremiah 29:12 – 13)

THE 10 COMMANDMENTS

1 You shall have no other Gods before me.

2 You shall not make unto thee any graven image.

3 You shall not take the name of the Lord thy God in vain.

4 Remember the Sabbath day and keep it holy.

5 Honor thy father and thy mother.

6 Thou shalt not kill.

7 Thou shalt not commit adultery.

8 Thou shalt not steal.

9 Thou shalt not bear false witness against thy neighbor.

10 Thou shall not covet.

SONGS OF MY HEART

We Have Come This Far by Faith

https://divinehymns.com/

We've Come This Far by Faith,
Leaning on The Lord.
Trusting in His Holy Word.
He's Never Failed Us Yet.
Oh, Oh- Oh- Can't Turn Around,
We've Come This Far by Faith.
Don't Be Discouraged with Troubles in Your Life.
He'll Bear Your Burdens
And Move All Discord and Strife
Oh! We've Come This Far by Faith,
Leaning on The Lord.
Trusting in His Holy Word.
He's Never Failed Us Yet.
Oh, Oh- Oh- Can't Turn Around,
We've Come This Far by Faith

Leaning on the Everlasting Arms

What a fellowship, what a joy divine,
Leaning on the everlasting arms;
What a blessedness, what a peace is mine,
Leaning on the everlasting arms.

Leaning, leaning, safe and secure from all alarms;
Leaning, leaning, leaning on the everlasting arms.

Oh, how sweet to walk in this pilgrim way,
Leaning on the everlasting arms;
Oh, how bright the path grows from day to day,
Leaning on the everlasting arms.

Leaning, leaning, safe and secure from all alarms;
Leaning, leaning, leaning on the everlasting arms.

REFLECTIVE TRIVIA

_____, who art in heaven,

Hallowed be thy name.

Father, I stretch _____

_____.

Let the redeemed _____.

Surely goodness and mercy shall follow me _____

_____.

Now I lay me down to sleep, I pray the _____

_____.

Jesus is on the main line _____

_____.

ANNIE WATTS
DEVOTIONAL

*L*OVING *&* DISCOVERING CONTENTMENT

"I have learned how to be content with whatever I have."
(Philippians 4: 11 NLT)

Contentment is not a virtue in our competitive culture. Ads drive us to want things we didn't even know existed and as soon as we purchase the latest and greatest thing, an even better version comes along to eclipse it! We envy friends and neighbors who live in better homes, drive fancy cars, and seem to live better lives than we do.

Comparing ourselves to others plants the seeds of jealousy and covetousness deep in our hearts. We sense that contentment will bring true peace to our lives. But how can we attain it - and keep it? How do we become truly content?

Let's for a moment just think about these words of our Savior:

"Don't worry about anything; instead, pray about everything. Tell God what you need and thank Him for all He has done. Then you will experience God's peace, which exceeds anything we can understand. His peace will guard your hearts and minds as you live in Christ Jesus." (Philippians 4: 6,7 NLT)

God loves you! He has always loved you! He will always love you! Confess to Him the contentment - killing scenes of jealousy and worry. Thank Him for the forgiveness Jesus won for you on Calvary's cross. Ask Him to help you trust that He will provide for you in the very best ways. Then, invite the Holy Spirit to give you genuine peace.

Prayer:

Lord Jesus,
In You and only in You is true contentment found. Lord, keep me focused on Your everlasting love for me. *Amen*

ABOUT
$\mathscr{A}$NNIE WATTS

Meet Co-Author Annie Watts, a born-again believer who accepted Christ as her Savior at twelve. She is a member of Sycamore Hill Missionary Baptist Church, Interim Pastor, Dr. Tony Barr. At her church, she serves as a member of the Rosebud Usher Board. On Sunday morning, you will find her at her post of duty, welcoming guests into the house of God.

Over the years, she has been known as a kindhearted individual who loves God, supports others, and owns Simply Delicious Cakery in Greenville, North Carolina.

She received her undergraduate and master's degrees from East Carolina University, Greenville, North Carolina. She majored in Early Childhood Education and Elementary Education. She is a retired schoolteacher who taught in the

Pitt County School Public Schools and is a Certified Lifetime Master Teacher. She is employed at Wake Technical Community College Raleigh, North Carolina, as an Adult Basic Education Instructional Mentor.

She is the daughter of the deceased parents, Jack and Mamie Nicholson, and is the first of five children. She is married to Charles C. Watts, Jr. They have been blessed with four daughters, four sons, six grandchildren, two great-grandchildren, and a host of relatives and friends.

Quote:

"I have learned that people will forget what you said, People will forget what you did, but people will never forget how you made them feel." -Maya Angelo

 SAVIOR

BY JESSUITA WILLIAMS

Acknowledgements

I want to thank my hubby and kids for their encouragement and support; my Pastors, Pastor Ricky, Sr. and Dr. Brenda Harrell, for their leadership and instilling God's Word; Mother Florine Price for her wisdom and mentorship; LoccedbyK for my hairstyle for my author picture; my family, my Christ Worship Center Church (CWCC) family, and all of you for supporting this work of God!

"When my bones were being formed, carefully put together in my mother's womb, when I was growing there in secret, you knew that I was there and saw me before I was born. The days allotted to me had all been recorded in your book before any of them ever began." (Psalms 139:15-16)

God knew who I was before I was created. He even helped my parents name me. My first name is Jessuita, pronounced "Jess c ta" or "Ja c ta." I was named after Jesus, so that's the purpose of the "u" in my name. My mom thought of the spelling, but my father named me. How can a person who loved me enough to name me never help raise me? My parents divorced when I was about two or three years old. Thank you, Lord, for being my Father. You said in Psalm 68:5, "A father to the fatherless, a defender of widow, is God in His holy dwelling." But see, God had a plan for my life. Even back then, He knew I was called to be different and set apart.

I've been attending church ever since I can remember. I've served in the youth and young adult choir and as the Sunday school and youth choir secretary. I have won multiple oratorical contests for Sunday school conventions, performed on the praise dance team, and done many other things involving the church. I was also on the A or A/B honor roll and in honor classes. I'm not saying any of that to boast or brag. I thank God for my accomplishments and accolades, but I have one question: Did I "really" know Him? You can have all the accolades, titles, memberships, degrees, money, and so on, but those will not grow your relationship with God or get you into Heaven.

I got baptized when I was about 12 or 13 years old, but still, did I know Him? My mentality in those days was my work in the church would get me to Heaven. Don't get me wrong,

I enjoyed everything I did, but did I have a personal relationship with Him? No, I didn't. I didn't pray or read the Bible outside of church. If I prayed, it probably was to get me out of a bad situation, such as doing something wrong and praying not to get caught by my mom or my teacher. To know God, you shouldn't only pray when you're in trouble or doing wrong. You have to have "intimacy" with Him. In the words of my Pastor, Ricky Harrell, Sr., "God wants you to be "into me, see."

In other words, you must read about Him and get to know Him. You must get in His presence. You must ask the Holy Spirit to come in. Close off all distractions and open your mind, eyes, and heart. Open your mind to receive wisdom and knowledge of the Word. Open your eyes to help see what message(s) God wants you to see from the scriptures. Open your heart to receive what God is telling you-whether it's good or something you don't want to hear or do. Go to God with expectancy! Expect a blessing! Expect a breakthrough! Expect instructions! Once you finish being intimate and getting to know Him, you should feel better and be more knowledgeable than you started.

For example, think about when you started dating your significant other. Some of you may have started as friends. Some of you may have been strangers before dating. After the meeting, you exchanged phone numbers, went on dates, and courted each other (like some seasoned people say). In other words, you spent quality time together to get to know each other. Sometimes, you may have gone on double dates with other couples or invited your significant other to events or family functions. When you want to be intimate, you want to be alone with them. You may play soft music, dim the lights, have a candlelight dinner, etc., but it is just the two of you.

Well, God wants that same intimacy-just you and Him-with no distractions. You can play soft inspirational music, put on a lamp, and even wear nice, comfortable attire. Whatever way you prepare for your time with Him, it doesn't matter to God. Jesus said in Proverbs 8:17, "I love those who love me, and those who seek me find me." God wants some time with you with no distractions. He wants you to get to know Him for yourself. "But grow in the grace and knowledge of our Lord and Savior Jesus Christ. To him be glory both now and forever! Amen." (2 Peter 3:18)

Some of the things that came into my life as opposition were the things that God used to create opportunities for me to get to know Him. God uses difficult situations to advance us. They help us realize we need God in our lives. In the summer of 2012, I was a married, stay-at-home mother of two small kids and an online student. While home alone, my posture and heart shifted. I wanted to know more about God. I longed for Him. I could tell I meant it this time and felt it from the depths of my soul. I prayed to God and told Him I wanted "to know Him."

About a month or two later, I became deathly ill. It started with me being unable to keep any food down - crackers, ginger ale, and the B.R.A.T. diet (bananas, rice, applesauce, toast). Nothing! I was vomiting so much that I began vomiting my bowels. The local hospital thought I had a stomach virus, so they gave me nausea medicine, ran tests, and sent me back home. Then, when I got so weak that I could barely walk, they would prescribe vitamins to help restore the nutrients I'd lost. The going back and forth to the hospital lasted for about a month.

I was so weak and numb that I couldn't bathe myself, walk by myself, or do anything without assistance. I even had to sign my name at the hospital with an "x" using my left hand, and I'm right-handed. This was nothing I was used to! Other than headaches, colds, or minor illnesses, I had never been sick. I'd only stayed in the hospital to have my two kids. Being this weak and vulnerable was so new to me. My mom was a working, single mom and could not stop working at the time, but she checked on me. My aunt, a business owner, dropped everything and volunteered to move in with me and my family during this time. She cooked, cleaned, and helped take care of my kids. She told my husband to work and take care of me, and she would handle the kids and everything else around the house. She did all of that and at no cost! My husband stuck by me and did what he needed to do and more. I'm so grateful!

During this time, I never gave up or stopped having faith. Yes, I did get frustrated and tired, but thank God, I never blamed Him. I started reading scriptures to get to know Him. I also listened to gospel music, especially when I sat in the bathtub. That helped me to press on.

After a little over a month, we went to my mom's house, which was about two hours away. She was the one who suggested we go to ECU Health in Greenville, NC. I was so frail from losing so many nutrients that I was wheeled into the hospital. I was 33 years old and weighed 90 pounds at that point. The doctor told me it was good I came in when I did, or I would not have made it. They kept me running test after test for weeks until they discovered what was wrong. So many families and friends visited me while I was in the hospital and kept me encouraged.

Even after I was released from the hospital, I still had to follow up with different specialists to have more tests run. In February 2013, I had just turned 34 years old, and the doctor diagnosed me with an incurable disease - Multiple Sclerosis (M.S.). Mayo Clinic defines multiple sclerosis as a disease in which the immune system eats away at the covering of nerves. Resulting nerve damage disrupts communication between the brain and the body.

Then, in April 2013, my husband and I found out we were expecting our third child before I was to start the M.S. medicine. We had been trying before I became ill. Before my grandmother passed away in March 2013, she had asked about seeing our new baby. I only had a six and a nine-year-old at the time. I was happy about the pregnancy because we had been trying for some time, but I was also sad because this meant I couldn't start on the M.S. medication. The only thing I knew about M.S. was that it was no cure, and you could die. The doctor informed me I couldn't start the M.S. meds; however, most women felt better during pregnancy. She thought it had something to do with pregnancy hormones. I felt fantastic during my pregnancy. Our healthy, miracle baby was born December 18, 2013, but was due on my grandma's birthday-the same one who spoke of her before her death.

During those seasons, I realized, as Ephesians 1:11-12 MSG states, "It's in Christ that we find out who we are and what we are living for. Long before we first heard of Christ and got our hopes up, He had His eye on us, had designs on us for glorious living, part of the overall purpose He is working out in everything and everyone." It hasn't been easy. Since being diagnosed with M.S. in 2013, I have been blind in one eye twice; I've had a breathing tube and had to be airlifted from one hospital to another because of the severity of the illness, and some more health issues all due to M.S. and my weakened immune system.

Today, I am doing well. I work full-time and am back to my motherly and wifey duties. My doctor stated that if it wasn't for a little, he couldn't tell I had M.S. As I told him, that's because my M.S. doesn't stand for Multiple Sclerosis but "My Savior."

In conclusion, to know God is relational. It doesn't matter your past, background, accolades, or accomplishments; you still need to have a relationship with Him. You must read His Word, talk, and pray to Him daily "to know Him." Philippians 3:10-12 AMP says, "And this, so that I may know Him [experientially, becoming more thoroughly acquainted with Him, understanding the remarkable wonders of His person more completely] and [in that same way experience] the power of His resurrection [which overflows and is active in believers], and [that I may share] the fellowship of His sufferings, by being continually conformed [inwardly into His likeness even] to His death [dying as He did]; so that I may attain to the resurrection [that will raise me] from the dead. Not that I have already obtained it [this goal of being Christlike] or have already been made perfect, but I actively press on so that [perfection] for which Christ Jesus took hold of me and made me His own."

Just to Know You
written by Pastor Ricky Harrell, Sr.

(Singing) *"Just to know You. Just to know You so well. My greatest desire in all of the world is to know You, really know You."*

JESSUITA WILLIAMS
DEVOTIONAL

$\mathcal{T}$ASTE & SEE THAT I AM GOOD

"Taste and see that the Lord is good; blessed is the man who takes refuge in Him." (Psalm 34:8)

The more intimately you experience God, the more convinced you become of His goodness. He is the living one who sees you and longs to participate in your life. He is training you to find Him each moment and to bring a channel of His loving presence. Sometimes, His blessings come to you in mysterious ways, through pain and trouble. At such times, you can know His goodness only through your trust in Him. Understanding will fill you, but trust will keep you close to Him.

So, thank God for the gift of His peace, a gift of such immense proportions that you cannot fathom its depth or breadth. When He appeared to His disciples after the resurrection, it was peace that He communicated first of all. He knew this was their deepest need: to calm their fears and clear their minds. He also speaks peace to you, for He knows your anxious thoughts. He says, "Listen to me! Tune out other voices so that you can hear Me more clearly. I designed you to dwell in peace all day, every day. Draw near to Me; receive My peace." *"Don't worry about anything;*

Prayer:

Oh, Heavenly Father, I thank you for loving me so much. So much that You would want me to taste Your goodness. Thank You for allowing me the intimate moments I can share with You. Thank You for Your Peace, which brings about faith and trust in You, which I can only have if I take the time to get to know You. Thank You, for I have tasted, and I know that You are good! *Amen.*

ABOUT
*J*ESSUITA WILLIAMS

Jessuita "Cee Cee" Williams is an only child and the daughter of Isabelle Andrews. She is married to the love of her life, Derek Williams, whom she met on a cruise 20 years ago. They have three kids: Jakevion, Kiara, and Mikayla.

Jessuita works for the Department of Social Services and enjoys serving the community. She loves singing, dancing, and spending time with her family, friends, and church family. She attends Christ Worship Center Church in Parkton, NC, where her pastors are Pastor Ricky, Sr. and Dr. Brenda Harrell, and they believe in "Loving People God's Way!"

WALK BY FAITH

CHAPTER 9

CRAZY FAITH & PRAYER!

BY HEIDI CASTRO

An intimate oneness with Jesus and an understanding that nothing can shake. This is how I live my life now, but I haven't always. I know the difference, and I will never return to anything less!

I've been a Christian since age 15. I have participated in many Bible studies and taught Sunday school for over 30 years, but that doesn't mean I didn't make some mistakes. I surely did! My name means "battle maiden." When I found this out, I laughed so hard I cried! In his wisdom, God must have known this was meant to be. It still makes me laugh.

One of the things that I've learned over anything else is that I have to spend time in the Word and wholeheartedly trust and rely on the Holy Spirit. I wish I had tapped into this power earlier on! Knowing He is with me every day makes a big difference.

Reading or saying scriptures aloud is one of the best ways to affirm God's Word in my life and bind Satan as I'm doing it. It may sound odd initially, but I proclaim the Word often as I walk through my home, close the bathroom door, or drive. All day, every day. It is powerful and effective.

"We demolish arguments and every pretension that sets itself up against the knowledge of God, and we take captive every thought to make it obedient to Christ." (2 Corinthians 10:5)

The Word of God renews our minds. We can forbid thoughts of failure and defeat, based on Ephesians 4:23.

I have a nickname; Cinderella. She's my favorite princess. It's silly but fun. I believe she gets a bad rap. Yes, we see a beautiful young woman who appears to allow herself to be taken advantage of. Some might even call her weak. But let's look deeper. If you think about it, she shows a lot of self-control. She gets frustrated, even angry, yet keeps her cool. How many of us can say we've always done that? I know I can't. It is just a story that can equate to our lives. She dealt with many harsh realities and stayed true to herself. She was almost ready to give up at one point but was shown some grace and kept trying. It's a game changer when we discover how much Jesus loves us and wants what's best for us. We have overflowing strength when we believe we are overcomers and declare it!

We are overcomers!! I like to walk around and say that out loud. I do it with my hands raised unless I'm driving, and then I use one hand. "I am an overcomer, and I am overcome by the blood of the lamb and the word of my testimony." Revelation 12:11. One person's idea of being an overcomer may be very different than somebody else's, and that's okay. Whatever it is that you want to overcome, say it. Speak the world you want! I'm not saying it's a magic wand and that things will appear instantly. This isn't magic; it's spiritual strength. Even if the changes are just in you, it's worth it.

Many people struggle with anger issues or unforgiveness. This can be hard to let go of. But it's imperative for your well-being. Not only does Jesus ask us to forgive as we have been forgiven, but it frees us from bondage. We are the ones that suffer the most when we do not learn to release these things.

You don't have to memorize many scripture verses to have a close personal relationship with Jesus, but you do have to start somewhere. I feel the best way to do that is to talk with Him. Cry out to Him. Lay on your bed or the floor and cry out to Him if necessary. He hears our thoughts, of course, but He wants to listen to us in prayer! He desires to be our everything! Even on your darkest days, when you don't even believe the words coming out of your mouth, say them anyway. And often, it will transform your mind and your soul. You will have strength and power that you never dreamed you could have.

Surrendering to God is never defeat! Speak words of life and light. Your words will either bring blessing or curse. They can connect you to the source of God's limitless power or drag you down into places you should not be.

"I am submitted to God, and the devil flees from me because I resist him in the name of Jesus." (James 4:7). Also read John 10:27 and Hebrews 13:5-6.

"May the words of my mouth and the meditation of my heart be pleasing in your sight, o Lord, my rock and my redeemer." (Psalm 19:14)

This is crucial in my life. He will cover you with his feathers, and under His wings, you will find refuge; His faithfulness will be your shield and rampart. Psalm 91:4. With this one, I say it as a proclamation to the Lord. "YOU cover me with Your feathers, and under YOUR wings I find refuge; YOUR faithfulness IS my shield and rampart!" This has been pivotal in my walk with Him. I hope it will be for you!

Like many people, there have been situations in my life where I feel broken and almost unable to function. When my daughter passed away, this was one of those times. No matter how much scripture I knew or how long I'd been a Christian, it was overwhelming! I could barely breathe. The pain seemed insurmountable, yet God gave me strength, peace, and hope. It takes time. Faith was and is my only answer! We don't get over some things; we learn to go on.

Many years ago, when my marriage was crumbling, I thought, "That's it; I'm just done with all this. I guess I'll never have that again." It was a rough time in my life. I wish I could say I made perfect choices and decisions, and all was well. But that was not the case. So many things were happening at this time. I didn't lose faith, but I wasn't spiritually where I should've been. I knew God loved me, but thought maybe he wouldn't allow a U-turn this time. I was so wrong! Eventually, I turned my eyes back to the Lord. However, I was comfortable with the way things were going. My husband and I had a good friendship, and it constantly improved.

One day, while driving and praying, I felt the prompting of the Holy Spirit speaking to me, saying, "You pray for all of these things and everyone else, and yet you have not entirely given me your marriage for restoration." I remember being undone by this, and with tears in my eyes, I pulled off the road and surrendered it to God. Amazing things have happened ever since. It's all about steps and choices. There were unknowns and things I wasn't sure I wanted to release. I chose to trust the promptings and never look back. "For I know the plans I have for you," declares the Lord, "plans to prosper you and not harm you, plans to give you hope and a future." Jeremiah 29:11.

We need to stop recreating the past and enjoy things from each season we are in. We can't control the famine or the harvest; that's not our job. God says, "No eyes have seen, no ears have heard, and no mind has conceived what God has prepared for those who love him." 2 Corinthians 2:9.

Trust can be difficult! I was highly blessed to be raised by incredible parents who did nothing but encourage, build me up, and love me. In turn, I gave that to my children. However, I've known many people and worked with children who did not have that kind of childhood. Many of whom were abused in many ways. So, trusting other humans can be a massive issue for some people. Most of us know someone who suffers from anxieties and fears and who has dealt with things some of us can't even imagine. It's important to acknowledge and seek help, but most importantly, keep learning to trust God to heal and strengthen you.

We grow when we stay in faith. There will be favor, blessings, and growth that you cannot imagine. It's not just about having a positive attitude; it's about agreeing with God!

God is the fountain that never runs dry. Allow yourself to be refreshed and transformed by his healing love. Ask God to unclutter your mind. Ask daily if necessary. He will do it!

Philippians 4:6-7 is my saving grace! Do not be anxious about anything, but in every situation, by prayer and petition, with thanksgiving, present your requests to God. And the peace of God, which transcends all understanding, will guard your hearts and minds in Christ Jesus.

I believe in reading scripture out loud, as I've mentioned, and there are certain ones that I particularly need to say and read every day.

"In you, O Lord, I have taken refuge; let me never be put to shame; deliver me in your righteousness. Turn your ear to me, come quickly to my rescue; be my rock of refuge, a strong fortress to save me. Since you are my rock in my fortress, lead and guide me for your name's sake. (Psalm 31:1-3) This one is so powerful to me. While you're saying it, picture yourself surrounded by the protection of wings like eagles, with nothing able to harm you.

We need to reject rationality and dare to believe. In the last few years, I've rediscovered that the single most important relationship in my life is one that I have with my Lord and Savior.

The Bible says the Word of God is medicine to our mind, body, and soul. But we must keep taking it, which means we must keep reading it and allowing it to heal us.

Look up Isaiah 61:2-3—a fantastic example of beauty for ashes. Our relationship with Jesus should be like a river flowing through you. You can't hold it all for yourself; it has to be shared with other people.

When it comes to faith, we have to retrain our brains not to complain because faith and complaining do not live well together. When you feel like complaining, stop and start praising God. You will be pleasantly surprised at how quickly things turn around for you. Easier said than done, I know. Because it's in our human nature to complain.

Again, the power and strength of God himself, as the Holy Spirit, is a source that must be understood. Peace is not the absence of problems; it is knowing to the depths of your soul that you are not alone. Romans 8:11

"I leave the gift of peace with you—my peace. Not the kind of fragile peace given by the world, but my perfect peace. Don't yield to fear or be troubled in your hearts; be courageous!" (John 14:27)

One of the things that was so wonderful for me to learn when I was young was contentment. The Bible has a lot to say about it.

Some verses to look up are 1 Timothy 6:6-10, Hebrews 13:5, and 2 Corinthians 12:9-10.

It doesn't mean we are not to aspire or try harder to reach our goals, but there is peace when we truly learn to be content in our circumstances.

I pray you draw closer to Jesus and are blessed in all you do.

DEVOTIONAL

ESIRES

"Delight yourself in the Lord, and He will give you the desires of your heart." Psalms 37:4

It's a fact of life that you don't always get what you want. The heart of a person is many, especially in a world that is geared toward self-fulfillment and gain. When your heart desires money, social media likes, and higher status more than it desires God, it's time for a heart check. Focusing our attention on God will mold our heart's desires to match His vision for us and how we can commit to spreading His love through our everyday interactions, whether on the campus, at work, in ministry, or while running errands. We must remember that God doesn't promise to fulfill your every craving, but if you live life in a relationship with Him, you will be satisfied - fully satisfied. As you grow in Christ, He will ultimately begin to wire you to look like Him and give you more of Him. When you grow in Him, your desires will evolve into God-ordained and purposed desires versus self-gain and ambition.

Prayer:

It's me, oh Lord, asking that You show me how to delight myself in You so that I might know what You desire for me and receive Your best for my life. I know Your promises are true, so I'll wait to hear from You. *Amen.*

ABOUT
Heidi Castro

I am a wife, mother, and grandmother. I love working with children and sharing Jesus. I enjoy helping my husband with his family martial arts association. I also enjoy reading, nature, walking, and crocheting. In the future, I plan to do more writing and speaking.

$\mathcal{N}$OT A STATISTIC: GRACED TO BREAK THE CYCLE

BY DANYEIL SHEPHERD

The Beginning

-42% of all children living in a single-parent household are considered poverty-stricken. (U.S. Census Bureau, 2018).

-1.4 million children reside in single-parent households that abuse alcohol. (U.S. Department of Health and Human Services, 2014).

-71% of children from fatherless homes dropout of high school, leaving these children nine times more likely to abandon their education. (National Principals Association Report on the State of High Schools, 2020).

This is how the world determined my outcome, growing up in a single-parent home. In reality, there are some things we do have to admit that affected us in childhood, and we dare to address them, but we do not have to let them define us. I appreciate a wonderful community and therapist who helps me navigate areas of my life that aren't perfect. I am also appreciative and indebted to God for not allowing the world's statistics to define and completely overtake me! Here's my faith story:

Danyeil Shepherd. The only girl who grew up with five brothers in Queens, New York. I've had great moments in my childhood where I enjoyed playing sports with friends and my brothers often. I particularly remember living above my grandfather's church, Christian Universal, where my family attended. On Sundays after church, my mom allowed my friends to come upstairs and play Nintendo video games, hide and seek, eat snacks, and run wild. It was a way to release all the energy we suppressed from sitting still for so long in Sunday morning service. The anticipation of knowing what was ahead felt like we all had personal implosions! Good times!

As you can imagine, growing up with all boys, I was more prone to playing sports and loved it! My first love was basketball. I played for my community in East Elmhurst, Queens, and was on the high school varsity basketball team. I was becoming such a star player that I considered joining the WNBA one day. However, once I started college, I focused more on my academics.

I remember always helping my youngest brother with his homework, and he always asked me to draw for him whenever he had to complete a project. I was always so proud and happy that I could help him. My youngest brother is seriously one of my best friends to this day.

My life in a snapshot was normal. However, although I had "normal" childhood moments and experiences, what others couldn't see was the reality of a broken family that I would go home to every day! I was born out of wedlock and witnessed my parents commit to each other in marriage. As I grew older, I began to understand their brokenness as they interacted with each other. I have also witnessed family members become incarcerated.

The History

My mother grew up in the foster care system, where she did not have the benefit of experiencing what healthy love, communication, and marriage looked like. Although my father experienced life with his biological mother, she was also a single mother. He had an estranged relationship with his father, so he also did not have a model of healthy relationships. As a result, I was 12 years old when my parents divorced, and our household then became a single-parent home.

One day, after coming home from a youth revival, I expressed to my mother how I believed God healed me from hurt and disappointment as it related to the divorce. Although very happy about my experience, my mother was also taken aback. My mother then stated that she thought she was shielding us from all the heated arguments and unhealthy communication between them, but I lovingly let her know that that was not the case. I heard, witnessed, and absorbed all of it!

Living in a single-parent home was not easy. I saw the hurt in both my mother and father. I was more acquainted with the hurt in my mother than I was with my father because my mother had full custody of me and my youngest brother, Dana. I saw the tears she cried when she thought I wasn't looking. I witnessed how she struggled financially, trying to make ends meet while also trying to attend to her needs. She often neglected her needs and wanted to ensure her children were cared for.

Although my mother struggled to be a single mother, she had an undeniable relationship with God! I would hear her worshiping and praying in her room, and she trusted God in every test and trial! I have witnessed God move for her financially, physically, & emotionally! My mother's faith in God kept us! She ensured that we were around Godly environments, such as church, youth events, bible studies, etc. Consequently, I could reap the benefits of my mother's prayers and faith in God! I could cultivate my relationship with God and build a Godly community around me that influenced and changed my life forever!

The Turn

At 14, I submitted my life to God wholeheartedly and began to watch Him work in my life! God began to deal with my heart about my relationship with my father. I was angry towards him because I was disappointed he was not around to help my mother. However, God began to soften my heart and strengthened me to forgive him. I remember praying this specific prayer: "Lord, please help my father become a better father." God heard me, and not only did He help my father become a better father, but He also worked on my heart. Sometimes, I refused to spend time with him on the weekends because I was so angry at him. My youngest brother would go, but often I would refuse to go. As God began to heal my heart and strengthen me to forgive, my relationship with my father couldn't be more assertive! Now, I am the ultimate "Daddy's Girl!"

God also began to put the right people on my path to live life with me! I cultivated a long-lasting sisterhood with my best friend, Denise, from age 14. I was also blessed to be discipled and mentored by my Youth Leader, Evangelist Vandalyn Kennedy, during this time. Our bond grew, and she ultimately became my Godmother. Through these initial relationships outside my parents and siblings, I began to know what my relationship with God could be like. I have modeled before me a life of pursuing higher education. My sister, Denise, is about three years older than me, so I witnessed her graduate from high school, travel, and pursue a college education. My Godmother, Vandalyn, had already obtained her Master's degree from Ivy League universities and had a career in education, and she also showed me how important it is to travel and broaden my horizons.

God used these influences in my life to help shape my thinking, and I also wanted to pursue higher education. Statistically, a child who grows up in a single-parent home is unlikely to achieve and obtain higher education. However, God graced me to defy the odds! I graduated from high school and was accepted into the University of Virginia, one of my top choices! Although I chose to attend Queens College instead (long story, lol), I became the first person in my immediate family to attend college and graduate with my Bachelor's Degree! I then went on to earn my Master's in Social Work at New York University. God is *AMAZING!*

I have watched God do great things, and I am eternally grateful! I am a Youth Minister, educator, non-profit owner, and entrepreneur. I have developed a great passion for mentoring and working with young people because of the impact mentoring had on my life growing up! One of my life's goals is to pay it forward to the next generation! At 34 years old, God didn't stop there! I became the first to own a home amongst my siblings. This step was the beginning of creating generational wealth and breaking the cycle of poverty and financial struggles in my bloodline.

Although the odds were stacked against me, God had other plans! If He can do it for me and grace me to defy the odds, He most certainly can do it for you! I was not supposed to achieve what God allowed me to achieve, but when God has a plan, nothing can stop it! God has graced me and continues to grace me to break generational cycles in my life. I am still walking by faith as I endeavor to pass these things along to my future children! Romans 8:31 says, "If God is for us, who can be against us?"

DEVOTIONAL

DO NOT NEGLECT YOUR GIFT

"Do not neglect your gift. Be diligent in these matters; give yourself wholly to them, so that everyone may see your progress." 1 Timothy 4:14-15

Viper most often refers to human abilities as gifts because they are given in order to be given again. If you have the gift of song, God expects you to strengthen and polish that gift and use it to enrich the lives of others. If you have been given a way with children, extend that gift to every child you meet. As you use your gifts to bless others, you will be blessed most of all.

There's a great scene at the beginning of The Equalizer where a young lady named Teri asks Robert (The Equalizer) what happens in "The Old Man and the Sea." Robert tells her that the old man catches the fish. She asks, "Why didn't he just let the fish go?" Robert replies, *"Old man's gotta be the old man. Fish has got to be the fish. Gotta be who you are in this world, no matter what."* In the context of the movie, it's not a statement of fatalistic resignation. It's also not parroting some silly version of, "You are perfect just the way you are!" Robert was pointing out that we are all made for a purpose, with a role to play. We have to find that purpose and live it.

It's an acknowledgment that we are made for some things and not others.

Prayer:

Thank you, Lord, for my gift. Let me not be selfish; let me always be willing to share with others what you have blessed me with. *Amen.*

ABOUT
*D*ANYEIL SHEPHERD

Danyeil Shepherd grew up in Queens, NY, with five brothers, being the only girl amongst her siblings. She accepted Christ as her Savior at the age of fourteen and has been on her faith journey ever since.

Danyeil has been serving in youth ministry from a teenager for 20 years, carried out various leadership roles, and God saw fit to promote her to leadership in 2021. She is an educator, entrepreneur, and non-profit business owner. She is also a mentor to young adults and young leaders. Danyeil founded 180 Impact, Inc., a summer program dedicated to cultivating the next generation of leaders and influencers through various group mentoring sessions. She also holds a Bachelor's and Master's degree from Queens College and New York University, respectively. Danyeil was the first in her family to enroll in higher education.

CHAPTER 11

*W*ALK BY FAITH

BY DR. MILDRED SUMMERVILLE

Walking by faith has been an incredible journey filled with valuable lessons and transformative experiences. While it has not always been easy, I understand that moments of doubt, fear, and uncertainty are opportunities for growth and strengthening my faith. In these challenging times, I have learned to lean on God's promises and find solace in His unwavering presence. Through these trials, I have discovered the true depth of my faith and the power of surrendering control.

Letting go and trusting in God's perfect timing has become a cornerstone of my journey. I have learned that His plan is far greater than anything I could ever imagine, and in embracing this truth, I have found a newfound sense of peace and contentment.

Patience has become a virtue that I strive to cultivate, and I have witnessed the beauty of divine orchestration unfold in my life. Each step of my journey has been intricately woven together, leading me down a path filled with purpose and fulfillment. Walking by faith has taught me the importance of perseverance, resilience, and unwavering trust in God's guiding hand. It is a profound testament to the power of faith and the incredible things that can be achieved when one walks in alignment with God's purpose.

My intention is not only to inspire and uplift others but to ignite a spark within their hearts, encouraging them to embrace their faith, discover their purpose, and live a life of impact and fulfillment. I hope to convey the message that with unwavering trust in God, anything is possible, and a life of purpose and meaning awaits those who dare to walk this path. I believe that each person has a unique calling, a divine purpose intricately woven into the fabric of their being, waiting to be uncovered and embraced. By sharing my own journey of faith and purpose, I aim to guide others towards self-discovery, encouraging them to listen to the whispers of their soul and embark on a transformative journey towards a life filled with passion, joy, and the unwavering knowledge that they are walking in alignment with God's divine plan. It is my deepest desire that through the words written, hearts will be stirred, spirits will be uplifted, and lives will be forever changed as individuals embark on a journey of faith, purpose, and the realization of their true potential.

Reflecting on my journey, I am humbled and deeply grateful for the countless blessings that have come my way. I placed my trust in God every step of the way, and He never failed me. My challenges, doubts, and uncertainties served as opportunities for growth and resilience. They tested my faith, pushing me to rely on God's strength and guidance. Through it all, I remained steadfast, walking by faith and becoming a woman of purpose. I have learned that despite adversity, there is a more excellent plan at work. The setbacks and disappointments I experienced were not setbacks at all but rather stepping stones toward personal growth and self-discovery. They taught me valuable lessons about perseverance, determination, and the power of faith. I learned to embrace uncertainty and have faith that everything happens for a reason.

One of the most profound realizations I have had on this journey is that my purpose extends far beyond my individual success. It is not solely about achieving personal goals or accumulating accolades. Instead, it is about utilizing my gifts and talents to make a positive impact on the lives of others. It is about being a vessel through which God's love and grace can flow, touching hearts and inspiring change. This understanding has driven me to seek opportunities to serve and uplift others within my career as an educator and beyond. I believe that true fulfillment comes from making a difference in the world and leaving a lasting legacy of kindness and compassion. It is not enough to exist and achieve personal success; we are called to go beyond ourselves and contribute to the well-being of others. By recognizing the value and potential in each individual, I strive to create an environment where everyone feels seen, heard, and supported.

As an educator, I have the privilege of shaping young minds, instilling knowledge, and nurturing a love for learning. But my role goes beyond academics. I strive to be a role model, teaching subject matter, life skills, empathy, and resilience. I aim to ignite curiosity, encourage critical thinking, and inspire a sense of purpose in my students. By fostering a safe and inclusive environment, I aim to empower them to embrace their strengths, pursue their passions, and positively impact the world. However, my commitment to serving others extends beyond the classroom. I actively seek opportunities to volunteer, support charitable causes, and lend a helping hand to those in need. Whether it is through mentoring, community service, or acts of kindness, I am dedicated to making a tangible difference in the lives of others. Even the smallest gestures of compassion and generosity can have a ripple effect, creating a chain reaction of positivity and transformation. I strive to be guided by love, empathy, and a deep sense of purpose in all that I do. I am humbled by the opportunity to be a vessel through which God's love and grace can touch the lives of others. I am committed to using my skills, passion, and resources to create a better world for future generations. I hope to leave a lasting legacy of kindness, compassion, and positive change by embracing my purpose and dedicating myself to serving others.

In my role as an educator, I have witnessed firsthand the transformative power of faith. I have seen students once disengaged and struggling to find hope and purpose by believing in something greater than themselves. The presence of faith in their lives has helped them overcome obstacles, develop resilience, and navigate challenges with grace. It has provided them with a sense of belonging and a moral compass to guide their decisions. Faith has instilled in them a deep sense of values and a commitment to serving others. I have witnessed a nurturing and inclusive educational environment's profound impact on a student's growth and development. We create an atmosphere of acceptance, love, and support by creating a space where faith is celebrated and embraced. Students feel seen, heard, and valued for who they are, allowing them to thrive academically, socially, and emotionally. It is a joy and privilege to witness young minds flourish and reach their full potential, guided by the light of faith. As an educator, I strive to create opportunities for students to explore and deepen their faith, ask questions, seek answers, and develop a personal relationship with God. I aim to foster an atmosphere of open dialogue where students feel comfortable sharing their beliefs and perspectives and where they can learn from one another's experiences. I believe that faith and education go hand in hand, as they both provide a foundation for personal growth, critical thinking, and a sense of purpose.

By integrating faith into the curriculum and classroom discussions, I aim to inspire students to see the world through a lens of compassion, justice, and love. I want them to understand that their faith is not separate from their education but rather an integral part of who they are and how they engage with the world. Ultimately, my goal as an educator is to empower students to become confident, compassionate, and resilient individuals who use their education and faith to impact their communities positively and beyond. I want them to leave my classroom with a deep sense of purpose and a commitment to live out their faith in meaningful ways. By nurturing their spiritual growth alongside their academic development, we can equip the next generation of leaders with the tools they need to create a more just, compassionate, and inclusive world.

Beyond the walls of the school, my faith has led me to become deeply involved in the community, driven by a desire to create opportunities for others to shine. As a firm believer in the power of artistic expression, I have taken it upon myself to organize and produce impactful events that provide platforms for aspiring artists to showcase their gifts and pursue their dreams. One such endeavor was the production of the play Spare the Rod, Spoil the Child, where talented actors and actresses were given the chance to bring their characters to life and captivate the audience with their performances. Additionally, I spearheaded the Wilson Idol talent show, a thrilling competition that allowed singers, dancers, and musicians to showcase their talents in front of a supportive and enthusiastic audience. These initiatives not only provide individuals with the opportunity to express themselves creatively but also serve as catalysts for bringing the community together. By fostering a sense of unity and celebration of talent, these events create a vibrant and inclusive environment where everyone feels valued and inspired. Through my faith-driven endeavors, I have witnessed firsthand the transformative power of art and its ability to uplift, inspire, and connect people from all walks of life.

Walking by faith has been an incredible and transformative journey that has shaped me in ways I never imagined. It has been a path filled with valuable lessons and profound experiences, challenging me to grow and strengthen my faith in the face of doubt, fear, and uncertainty. In those moments of darkness, I have learned to lean on God's promises and seek solace in His unwavering presence. Through these trials, I have discovered the true depth of my faith and the power of surrendering control to a higher power. Letting go of my own expectations and trusting in God's perfect timing has become a cornerstone of my journey. I have learned that His plan for my life is far greater than anything I could ever conceive, and in embracing this truth, I have found a newfound sense of peace and contentment. Patience, once a virtue I struggled to cultivate, has become a guiding principle. I have witnessed the beauty of divine orchestration unfold as each step of my journey has been intricately woven, leading me down a path of purpose and fulfillment. Through the highs and lows, walking by faith has taught me the importance of perseverance, resilience, and unwavering trust in God's guiding hand. It is a journey that continues to unfold, and I am grateful for the lessons it has taught me.

As I continue on this path of purpose, my heart overflows with gratitude. I am thankful for the abundance of opportunities that have come my way, each one serving as a catalyst for personal growth and transformation. Through these experiences, I have gained valuable lessons and wisdom, equipping me with the resilience and strength needed to navigate the challenges that await me. But amidst it all, my unwavering faith has been my guiding light, providing me with hope, courage, and a sense of purpose. I am also profoundly grateful for the unwavering support and belief of those who have stood by me, encouraging me to reach for the stars and reminding me of the power of love and community. Amid this journey, I am humbled by the divine guidance that has led me to where I am today, the synchronicities and signs that have reassured me that I am on the right path. With gratitude in my heart, I embrace the future with open arms, knowing that I am not alone and eagerly anticipating the adventures that lie ahead.

DR. MILDRED SUMMERVILLE
*D*EVOTIONAL

$\mathcal{A}$CCOMPLISHMENT

"Commit your Works to the Lord, and your plans will be established." Proverbs 16:3

Whatever God has called you to accomplish in your life, He has not called you to accomplish it alone. He is always there, providing you with the resources you need to get the job done. That doesn't mean you won't stumble along the way or encounter difficulties. But it does mean that you can call upon the council and resources of the almighty God to help you. Whether you need wisdom, inspiration, confidence, strength, or just plain tenacity, you will find your answer in Him.

$\mathcal{P}$rayer:

Father, help me to accomplish anything that I set my mind to do. I know there will be obstacles, but nothing that you can't help me to get through. Father, guide me; grant unto me Your wisdom, Your grace, and Your strength. *Amen.*

ABOUT
*M*ILDRED SUMMERVILLE

Dr. Mildred Summerville, hailing from Wilson, North Carolina, is a creative force with a journey marked by acclaim. With a strong educational background, including a B.S. from Fayetteville State University, an M.Ed. from Bowling Green State University, and a Principal's Certificate from East Carolina University, Dr. Summerville is a trailblazer in the field of education.

Driven by her faith, Dr. Summerville has received several prestigious honors, including a Doctorate of Humane Letters in 2011 and an Honorary Doctorate in Humanitarianism in 2019. Currently serving as the International Chaplain and Matriarch for GIA, North Carolina Division, she has held diverse roles, including coach and playwright.

Dr. Summerville's notable achievements include founding the James and Leanther Summerville Academy, a testament to her dedication to education. She has also received the President's Lifetime Achievement Award and established Tall One Outreach Ministries, showcasing her commitment to community service.

Affectionately known as the "Tall One" by Dr. Shirley Caesar, Dr. Summerville's impressive height of six feet is just one aspect of her larger-than-life presence. Her gospel play, "Spare the Rod, Spoil the Child," has garnered widespread acclaim, earning her the Playwright & Gospel Stage Play of The Year Award.

Recognized for her impactful contributions, Dr. Summerville has received over 30 awards, including the President Biden Lifetime Achievement Award in 2021. Her book, "A Woman with a Vision," further showcases her passion for empowering young minds and leaving behind a lasting legacy of inspiration and service.

Dr. Mildred Summerville is a true inspiration. She embodies the power of education, playwriting, and community service. Her remarkable journey serves as a beacon of hope for future generations.

$\mathcal{A}$MEN

Made in the USA
Columbia, SC
06 January 2025